ABUL HASAN ALI NADWI

THE GLORY OF IQBAL
1877
1938

> Even as I depart from this world,
> Everyone will say, "I knew him,"
> But the truth is, alas! That none knew,
> Who the stranger was, or what he said, or whence he came!
>
> — Iqbal

ABUL HASAN ALI NADWI

THE GLORY OF IQBAL
1877
1938

Abul Hasan Ali Nadwi

TRANSLATED BY
M. ASIF KIDWAI

1 2 3 4 5 6 7 8 9 10

Claritas Books
Bernard Street, Swansea, United Kingdom
Milpitas, California, United States

© Claritas Books 2018

This book is in copyright. Subject to statutory exception and to the provisions of relevant collective licensing agreements, no reproduction of any part may take place without the written permission of Claritas Books.

First Edition: May 2002
Second Edition: September 2007

Typeset in Bembo 11/14

The Glory of Iqbal
by Abul Hasan Ali Nadwi
Translated by M. Asif Kidwai

A CIP catalogue record for this book is available from the British Library

ISBN: 9780953758296

Special thanks to
Wali, Omar, Nicola, Thaherah

SHAYKH ABUL-ḤASAN ʿALĪ NADWĪ was born in India in 1914. He belonged to the illustrious family of Syed Ahmed Shahid (1786-1831). Shaykh Nadwī excelled in the studies of *tafsīr*, hadith and *fiqh*. He mastered the Arabic language and literature to the extent that in the years to come most of his books would be written in Arabic. He was the rector of Darul Ulum Nadwatul Ulama and president of the Academy of Islamic Research & Publications. He was the founding member of Rabita al-Alam al-Islami (Muslim World League) and vising professor at the Universities of Damascus and Madinah respectively. He was the founding member of Oxford Centre for Islamic Studies, and in 1980 he was awarded the King Faisal Award for his services to Islam. He passed away in 1999.

CONTENTS

	INTRODUCTION	XI
	FOREWORD	XIX
1	Biographical Sketch	1
2	Formative Factors	9
3	Western Civilisation	23
4	Modern Education	35
5	Knowledge and Learning	45
6	Art and Architecture	51
7	The Perfect Man	63
8	The Place of the True Believer	75
9	Satan's Advisory Council	81
10	To the Arab Lands	95
11	The Mosque of Cordoba	103
12	Ardour and Eagerness	113
13	The Problem of Palestine	119
14	In Afghanistan	123
15	The Prayer of Ṭāriq	129
16	To the Saqi	133
17	The Lamentation of Abū Jahl	141
18	Echo of Paganism	147
19	With Jamāluddīn Afghānī	151
20	At the Doorstep of the Prophet ﷺ	159
21	Complaint and Prayer	171
22	Historical Truths and Allusions	179
	NOTES	193

INTRODUCTION

> Even as I depart from this world,
> Everyone will say, "I knew him,"
> But the truth is, alas! That none knew,
> Who the stranger was, or what he said, or whence he came!
>
> *Muhammad Iqbal*

Shaykh Abul-Ḥasan ʿAlī Nadwī comes from a family that has been at the centre of learning and literature, guidance and instruction, uninterruptedly, for hundreds of years. All these attributes are richly represented not only in his personality, but also throughout his religious, literary and academic endeavours. The extraordinary command that the Shaykh possesses over the Arabic language and his thorough and wise understanding of the spiritual and cultural problems of the Muslim world have lent great weight and importance to his views, and are thus unequalled by any other Muslim theologian of modern India. The Shaykh can thus be described as the most distinguished ambassador of the Muslim *Millet*.

Shaykh Nadwī is in all probability the first religious scholar to have keenly and enthusiastically studied the life and thought of Iqbal, who was indubitably the greatest and most representative Urdu poet of the 20th century. It is essential for the *ʿulamāʾ* (scholars) themselves to now try to understand Iqbal as both life and religion are going to be viewed and evaluated in the manner and context laid down by him. The Shaykh is aware of the needs and urges of the modern mind and gives them attention and respect, his attitude being identical to another celebrated product of the Nadwa, Syed Sulaiman Nadwi.

It is not easy to appreciate the collective mental, moral, social and spiritual qualities of the *Millet* and the worth and value of the gifts bestowed by it upon mankind without a serious and respectful study of Hali and Iqbal. The benefaction of the love of the Prophet has indeed invested their works with immortality. *Na't-goi*[1] is a difficult and sublime art and act of devotion and is as majestic and benevolent as is the personality to which it owes its existence. It is admitted even by a poet like 'Urfi who, in his poetical self-conceit, cares little for anyone's position of superiority, but with regards to *Na't* he emphasises the need of caution and wakefulness at each step.

> Hurry not, O 'Urfi, it is the pathway of the Na't.

Or,

> Slowly! Thou art treading on the edge of the sword.

And again,

> Beware! One cannot on the same harp sing,
> Praises of the Prophet, and eulogy of Cyrus, Jamshed.

It is not a characteristic of the poets alone, but for every Muslim, his religious and cultural worthiness is the extent to which his life and character are imbued with warm affection for the Prophet ﷺ. Whilst we are indebted to *Milad-Namas* and *Milad-Khwans*[2] for the concept of love of the Holy Apostle, we must also credit Hali and Iqbal, as they accomplished the task of changing such a concept from an emotional sensation to that of a living desire so that we could understand, acquire and preserve the high ideals of Islam and the *Millet*. The ability to respect and observe the commands of God and the sacred Apostle is a Divine gift, but to explain and publicise such instructions and to impress them upon the hearts and minds of people has become the duty of the inspired poets to whose "sweet word" Iqbal has alluded in

Introduction

his unique style in the following verse:
> Gabriel is Yours, Muḥammad Yours, Yours the Quran,
> But this sweet word, Your interpreter or mine?

This is great poetry, which is undying and imperishable like the Holy Scriptures, and it is their creature as well as their interpreter. It blends religion with culture and culture with religion and the two with life and keeps them fresh, integrated and dynamic. The place of Iqbal in Urdu poetry is similar. The fervour and sincerity with which Hali in *'Arz-i-Haal* and *Musaddas* and Iqbal in *Zarb-i-Kalim* and some other poems cry to the "noblest of the noble Apostles." They are seen in the presence of the "mark of Mercy" and belong to the realm of higher literature, not only in Urdu, but in world poetry. Fortunately, the honour of carrying Iqbal's message to the Arabs, in the Arabic language, has gone to Shaykh Nadwī!

A correct idea of the charm and brilliance with which the Shaykh has expressed his views and feelings on the life and art of Iqbal and on some of his most popular poems and Urdu masterpieces, particularly, *Armughan-i-Hejaz,* can be obtained from *Nuqoosh-i-Iqbal*[3] or *Rawa-i-Iqbal*.[4] The sands of Arabia, "soft as silk under our feet," the imaginary journey by Iqbal to the blessed city of Madinah, the trotting of the camel on the pitch and tone of "Hurry not, for the destination is near," the ecstatic representation of innermost thoughts and sentiments in different ways and the coaxing of the camel to tread in harmony with them—the ability to cast all this into exquisite Arabic, while preserving the emotional richness of the whole event, of trotting and conversing, testifies to the wonderful mastery of the Shaykh over Arabic expression and idiom.

Long ago, I had an opportunity to hear a talk by Allama Iqbal at Lahore. It went something like this: Why was Islam revealed in Arabia? The Allama observed that the desert-wandering Arabs were never civilised. Since civilisation eventually led to the downfall of a people, the trust of Islam could not be placed in the hands of a community that could fall prey to the wastefulness and luxury that inevitably followed in its wake. Thus, whenever Muslims outside Arabia would be caught up in decay and ruin they would look to that desert land and its sturdy, nomadic people for warmth, light and movement. Today, this statement comes to my mind, "I have nothing against the Bedouin Arabs, of whose boats the sea was a playground." However, the vulgar ostentation of their rulers and other privileged classes and the extent to which they have fallen in the esteem of the world is extremely shameful and distressing.

All the same, it is a source of encouragement that the religion which once had "invited Caesar and Chosroes" and whose followers had conveyed the message of peace, truth and generosity to the four corners of the world is now being revived and taken back to the Arabs through the "son of a Syed," someone who was born in a Brahmin home and whose ancestors used to worship the idols. It remains to be seen how not only the Arab countries but also the entire Islamic world responds to it and it derives freshness and vitality from the soul-stirring declaration that the "Arab World" is from "Muḥammad of Arabia." Did the remark made by the Leader of the Arabs (the Holy Prophet) that, "I feel a cool breeze coming from the direction of Hind" really convey this wonderful circumstance? But who can tell what the concept of the Arab World is among the Arabs? Is it of Muḥammad of Arabia or of Arab disunity and misrule?

Like the *Na't* of the sacred Prophet, the new dimension and sublimity Iqbal has given to the tragedy of Karbala and martyrdom of Imām Ḥusayn also makes a valuable contribution to Urdu poetry. He experimented with the significance of the composition and recitation of Marsia[5] in our life and literature and gives a new validity to it. A new symbol of "the station of the Shabbir"[6] was thus introduced in Urdu literature and it became immediately popular. A previously limited concept has now become limitless.

> Sands of Iraq are waiting; Arabia's sowing-field is thirsty,
> To Kufa, Syria and Egypt give again the blood of Ḥusayn.
> Strangely plain and colourful is the story of *Ḥaram*,
> Its beginning is Ismāʿīl, Ḥusayn the end.
> The station of Shabbir is truth everlasting,
> Ways of Kufa and Syria change from time to time.
> Not one Ḥusayn in the caravan of Hejaz is found,
> Tresses of Tigris and Euphrates though are lustrous still.
> Love is the truthfulness of Khalīl; fortitude of Ḥusayn is love,
> In the battle of life, Badr and Ḥunayn are love.

A vivid description of the injustice that has generally been suffered by women and the woeful disregard of their honour and welfare is found in the poems of Hali and Iqbal. Moreover, Iqbal feels that the improper use to which they have been applying liberty, which has come to them owing to the sudden removal of restraints after two World Wars, is based in their permissiveness. Having said that, it is impossible to disagree with what he says in their praise and glorification in *Zarb-i-Kalim* and other poems

> Colour in the portrait of Universe is from woman,
> From her warmth the inner warmth of life;
> In glory her dust is greater than Plaedias,
> Each glory is the hidden pearl of her shell.
> Dialogues of Plato she could not write,
> Yet Plato's spark by her flame was broken.

At the end of *Rumuz-i-Bekhudi,* the poet declares the human race to be dependant on motherhood and upholds "the way of Hazrat Fāṭimah" as the perfect model for Muslim women to aspire to for three reasons: Firstly, she is the daughter of the Prophet ﷺ, "the Mercy to the Worlds." Secondly, she is the wife of ʿAlī Murtuza, "the disperser of difficulties." And thirdly, she is the mother of Imām Ḥusayn, "the leader of martyrs." It would be difficult to find a more enlightened guide to the rights and duties of women anywhere.

Such verses, lines and phrases, in which Iqbal has commented on the various problems, events and personalities of his own and the earlier times have been brought to fruition with superb skill and amazing insight and constitute an invaluable addition to Urdu poetry. This voice, style and distinctiveness is rarely found among Urdu poets whose works sometimes include laboriously composed verses and even whole poems.

Iqbal's poetry is free from all that is redundant and superficial. It only goes to show just how evolved and original were his taste and mind, since he could effortlessly transform the commonplace into the exceptional. Being so conscious of the superior, he found himself unable to settle with anything less.

I wonder how Urdu poetry would have been viewed these days, in a time when all the traditional values are being distorted or rejected, had it not been for Ghalib, Hali, Akbar, and Iqbal and the solidity and permanence they gave it. In not only form and substance, but also in thought and theme and style and diction, Iqbal has set a standard that is not easy to emulate.

Followers of a particular school are inclined to suggest that Iqbal preaches bloodshed and seeks to foist the individual on the society. It is an old criticism that can be answered easily. How can an ardent admirer of the "Mercy to the Worlds" (the Holy Prophet) support or advocate the dogma of cruelty and violence? As for Iqbal's deep devotion to the Prophet, ample evidence of it is available in *Nuqoosh-i-Iqbal*. Furthermore, in order to fully understand the nature of the relationship between the individual and society and their mutual obligations and responsibilities, one will have to study *Asrar-i-Khudi* and *Rumuz-i-Bekhudi* carefully. Iqbal has stressed a two-fold education of the individual; one is his capacity as an individual and the other as a member of the community. In other words, as long as the individual and the community remain divided and do not act together, in thought and in deed, for a noble purpose, a strong and healthy society can never come into being. Refinement, wisdom and ambition, upon which society depends for its existence and advancement, begin with the individual and end with the community. The instruction of both is aimed not at keeping them apart but at bringing them together and producing a common aim and purpose. Without the guidance and leadership of the individual society is bound to fail. It then becomes dangerous and pathetic. Education is imparted to the individual so that he can lead the community on the straight path, not so that he can make it an instrument of his selfish ends. The bond between individual and society, as envisaged by Iqbal, is such that it keeps them united and safe from each other's feelings of superiority.

In their support the critics cite some of Iqbal's verses in which he has spoken of the chasing of the pigeon by the falcon. "Charging, turning and charging again," or the worthlessness of leadership without power, "Without the rod, *Kalimi* is a meaningless act." In addition, critics ought also to keep in mind the warning that Iqbal never tires of giving us:

> On life's battleground develop the character of steel,
> In love's bedchamber become soft like silk.

Life and times being what they are, can there be a more reliable formula for living with peace, honour and freedom? Humility without strength is the virtue of a beggar. It is our duty to be strong. Misuse of force is cowardice and is another name for cruelty. The dispenser of difficulties is the individual, not the community. A conspicuous example in modern times of *Kalimi*[7] without the rod is the United Nations.

Shaykh Nadwī is an erudite scholar and an expert judge of literary and poetic merit. He also possesses an enlightened mind. His praise and elegant interpretation of Iqbal confirms the view that I have held for a long time, that his philosophy is part of the scholastic theology of the twentieth century and will remain fresh and sound for many years to come, as it has been cast in magnificent poetry. Iqbal's enlightened, scholarly and poetic exposition of the beliefs, practices and traditions of Islam has made a deep mark upon Muslim society. Such a healthy and purposeful awakening has rarely been brought about by the scholastic theology of any other period. Some people, undoubtedly, have not been moved so powerfully by reading religious books directly as by learning about the same truths through Iqbal's verses. This is evident in the fact that the Muslim theologians who were reluctant to accept some of the views expressed by Iqbal in his well-known lectures on *The Reconstruction of Religious Thought in Islam* became readily convinced of them when they read or heard about them in his poems, and it was as if those concepts and doctrines had been revealed to them straightaway.

I trust the Shaykh will not differ with me that the poetry of Iqbal is the scholastic theology of the present century.

Prof. Rasheed Ahmad Siddiqi

FOREWORD

Before I attained the age of adolescence Iqbal had established himself as a poet of distinction. Many of his verses had become household phrases. It is possible that no poet has captured the imagination of his generation as powerfully as Iqbal did. He had a tremendous impact on his age. It is not surprising, therefore, that I was drawn to his poetry while still young and remained attached to it ever after.

There can be many reasons why people like great poetry. The most important and common of these perhaps is that people find within it an experience similar to their own hopes and ideals. Man being basically egocentric, he is attracted by all that reflects his inner urges and speaks the language of his heart. I do not exclude myself from this. Perhaps, I admired Iqbal because I found him very close to my ideas and feelings and felt that through his verses he gave expression to what was really passing through my own mind. However, what attracted me most to his poetry was the message of love, high aspiration and faith that it carried, and this was rare in the works of contemporary poets. I feel instinctively drawn to any movement or literature that upholds the virtues of generosity and sincerity and calls for Islamic revival. Furthermore, in Iqbal's poetry I also found something that stimulated the desire for the development of self-hood and the conquest of "the inner and the outer worlds." This was in addition to promoting feelings of love and fidelity and encouraging religious consciousness and a deep faith in God and the greatness of Prophet Muḥammad and the universality and eternity of the message he brought. I admired Iqbal particularly as a champion of human equality and brotherhood, as envisaged in Islam, and a believer in the essential nobility of the Muslim. I also admired him as a fearless citric of the Western materialistic civilisation and a courageous fighter against a narrow-minded nationalism and crude parochialism.

I began reading his poetry while still a child, and as I grew up I tried to translate some of his verses into Arabic. I had only read the Urdu poems contained in his collection called *Bang-i-Dara* (*The Caravan Bell*). Meanwhile, two of his collections had appeared in Persian, but I had not yet learned to appreciate that language.

I met him for the first time in 1929, when I was sixteen years old. I was visiting Lahore, which at that time was a great centre of learning and culture. On a hot summer day, Dr. Abdullah Chughtai, Professor of Islamic Studies in the Punjab University introduced me to Iqbal, telling him that I was a keen admirer of his poetry. Dr. Chughtai also mentioned my father, the late Maulana Hakim Syed Abdul Hai Hasni, whom Iqbal knew well through his valuable book *Gul-i-P'Ra'ana* that had just been published and had become immensely popular in literary circles all over the country. In that meeting, I presented him with a copy of my rendering of his poem *Chand* ("The Moon") into Arabic. Iqbal was pleased to read it, and then he asked me a few questions about some Arab poets, probably to assess the extent of my scholarship. I came away greatly impressed by his simplicity, sincerity and humility.

During the period between 1929 and 1937, I often visited Lahore and stayed there for months. However, I did not feel like disturbing the great poet, believing that there was no need to hurry, as he would remain among us for a long time. Besides, I am rather shy of meeting great men, and my own pre-occupation with studying was also partly responsible for putting off the visit.

His other two collections of Urdu poems were published at that time. They appeared quite some time after the poet had stopped writing in Urdu and taken to Persian. Both of these volumes were richly representative of Iqbal's poetic genius and erudition. At that time I liked *Zarb-i-Kalim* (*The Stroke of the Rod of Moses*) more but later *Bal-i-Jibril* (*The Wing of Gabriel*) became my favourite and in this book I have drawn greatly from it.

At that time I was a teacher in Nadwat-ul-Ulema of Lucknow and used to share my room with the late Maulana Masood Alam Nadwi who was a distinguished scholar of Arabic and the editor of *Al-Zia,* brought out by the same institution in Arabic. We used to read Iqbal together as my late lamented friend was also an ardent admirer of the poet, and we both did not feel happy that Tagore was better known in the Arab World than he was. Tagore had found many admirers among scholars in Syria and Egypt and we felt that we were responsible. We had done nothing to introduce Iqbal to the Arabic-speaking peoples, so whenever we saw an Arabic journal praising Tagore and his poetry (and we used to read these journals regularly) our resolve to translate Iqbal's poems into Arabic grew stronger. We began to regard it as a duty and a trust.

It so happened that I had another meeting with the poet a few months before his death. It was a long meeting that is worthy of being remembered. On November 22, 1937, I visited Iqbal with my uncle, Syed Talha Al-Hasni, and his son, Syed Ibrahim Al-Hasni. By this time the poet was confined to his house owing to a long illness that ultimately proved fatal. Nevertheless, he welcomed us with great warmth and we stayed for over three hours. His old and devoted servant, Ali Bux, fearing that the strain might prove too much for him, came in a number of times in order to stop him from over-exerting himself, but the Allama ignored his advice and went on talking to us. He freely expressed his views on several subjects. Speaking of the pre-Islamic Arab poetry the poet remarked that he admired its realism and vitality and the spirit of chivalry and heroism that it breathed and even recited a few verses of *Hammasah*. He said that Islam prescribed its followers resolute action and love of reality and added that positive sciences were nearer to Islam because of their rejection of philosophical speculation.

For two centuries the Muslims kept this tradition alive and remained loyal in faith, morality and active endeavour. Then with the impact of mainly Hellenistic thought, the whole of the East became intellectually crippled. It became a "sick man." Iqbal remarked that the renaissance of Europe was possible only when it had thrown off the influence of Greek metaphysics and turned its attentions to useful and more productive branches of learning. However, in the present age many problems arose which made Europe become reactionary in its outlook. Iqbal felt that Hellenistic thought, unfortunately, did the same to Islam what it had done to Christianity in Europe. It overpowered both the religions.

With regard to Sufism (Islamic mysticism) Iqbal deplored the ideological excessiveness of the Muslim mystics and observed that while the Companions of the sacred Prophet took delight in horsemanship and martyrdom, the Sufis revelled in *Samā^c* (music) and *Wajd* (ecstasy). With regards to the resurgence of Islam in India, he praised the efforts of Sheikh Ahmad Sarhindi, Shah Waliullah Dehlavi and Emperor Aurangzeb. If it hadn't been for them and their endeavours, he said, Indian philosophy and culture would have swamped Islam.

He also spoke of the need of Pakistan (it should be noted that Pakistan was originally his idea which then materialised in 1947 after his death) and remarked that people without a homeland could neither preserve their faith nor develop their culture. The preservation of religion and culture was dependent on political power. Hence, Pakistan was the only solution to the problems and economic difficulties of Indian Muslims. In this connection he also referred to the Islamic institutions of *Zakāt* (regular charity) and *Baytu'l-Māl*.[8]

About the immediate future of Muslims in India, he told us that he had drawn the attention of some Muslim Princes to the need of preaching and propagation of Islam among non-Muslims. He had also been laying stress on the religious reform and uplift of Muslims, the promotion of Arabic language and the establishment of a World (Muslim) Bank. Moreover, it was necessary to have a first-class daily English newspaper of Muslims for supporting their cause and lending strength to their voice. Unfortunately, he sorrowfully added, the Princes did not take his advice. They did not appreciate the gravity of the situation and the significance of the changes that were taking place in the world. They were selfish, petty and short-sighted.

The poet wanted to go on with the conversation, but we felt that in view of his illness it would be better to depart, so we said good-bye to him and left. We came away from Lahore within a few days. This was our last meeting.

I distinctly remember that when I asked his permission to translate some of his poems into Arabic he expressed his pleasure and readily granted me his permission. I read him some of my Arabic renderings of verses from *Zarb-i-Kalim*. He told me that Dr. Abdul Wahab Azzam (of Egypt) also was thinking of translating some of his works. Six months later when I heard of his death, on April 21, 1938, my resolve to undertake a study of his life and art became firmer. I wrote to my friend, Maulana Masood Alam, who was then at Patna and after having exchanged condolences on the death of the magnificent poet, we decided to combine our efforts in order to carry out the task. He offered to write about the personality and message of Iqbal (for, as he said, he was not very good at translating) and left the translation of his poems into Arabic to me. The work thus began. Maulana Masood Alam wrote a stimulating article on Iqbal, which appeared in *Al-Fatah* of Cairo, a journal edited by my old friend, the late Mohibuddin Khatib. I also wrote an article on Iqbal's life, which was broadcast sometime after by the Saudi Arab Radio. However, due to various reasons the work then remained suspended for ten years.

In 1950, I visited Arabia, Syria and Egypt. During my stay of over a year, I wrote a few papers on Iqbal, his thought and his art, and read them at Dār al-ʿUlūma and the University of Fuad (now known as the University of Cairo). In 1956 in Syria, I wrote another article entitled, *Mohammad Iqbal in the Madinah of the Prophet,* which was broadcast by the Damascus Radio. However, I could not persuade myself to start translating Iqbal's poems. One of the reasons, perhaps, was that Dr. Abdul Wahab Azzam had already begun translating and owing to his mastery of both the Persian and Arabic languages and his intellectual relationship with Iqbal, I felt that he was possibly more suited for the job.

As a couple of collections of translations[9] saw the light of day, some of my friends said that they lacked Iqbal's warmth and sparkle and did not adequately convey his thought and message. They were, on the whole, not worthy of Iqbal's tremendous poetry. When I myself read them I felt that they did not suffer from any technical fault nor fail to understand Iqbal, rather, they were a convincing example of Dr. Azzam's command over Arabic expression. The main drawback with them was that by attempting to translate Iqbal, Dr. Azzam had failed to do justice both to himself and to the great poet.

A good deal of the force, vitality and effectiveness of Iqbal's poetry was lost in the process. In addition, a kind of vagueness and tortuosity had crept into the translation and had thus created a barrier between the reader and his response to the poetry. It would have been better if Dr. Azzam, who was a noted Arabic scholar and possessed a thorough knowledge of the Persian language, had first delved deeper into the art and thought of Iqbal and then translated his work in the form of prose as he had preferred for articles which had been published in the well-know Egyptian journals, *Ar-Risala* as *As-Siqafa*.

Every language has its own mood and flavour, its own idioms and ways of expression, the roots of which can be traced back in history and culture. If this is lost in translation, much of the charm and fire of the original text will be destroyed. Nevertheless, by translating some of Iqbal's poems into Arabic verse, Dr. Azzam has rendered a great service to Islam and to the Muslim literary world for which he deserves praise and the thanks of the scholars of Islamic thought and literature. The translation bears an eloquent testimony to his deep learning and sincerity and there is no doubt that Iqbal's soul will be happy over this labour of love.

My many activities and pre-occupations over-shadowed the desire of translating Iqbal till it was stirred by an event. I read an open letter addressed to me by the renowned Arab scholar, Dr. Ali Tantawi, in the pages of *al-Muslimūn*, in which he had asked me to introduce Iqbal to the Arab World. It read:

> Will you translate some selected poems of Iqbal into Arabic so that we can properly appreciate the greatness of his poetry and message? The few Arabic translations that are available have not succeeded in giving us a correct picture of Iqbal's structure of thought and the magnificence of his poetry. Will you, therefore, include this service among the tasks you have set before yourself and convey to the Arab World the freshness and fragrance of Iqbal's poetry which up to now has remained a stranger, and thus open the gates of this delightful garden for us also, and thus enrich the Islamic literature?

I could only respond to this appeal with enthusiasm. The translation of the poem, *Masjid-i-Qurtuba* ("The Mosque of

Cordova") was completed in one sitting and I felt a renewed urge to go ahead with the job, which was now impossible to ignore. This set the work in motion, and soon a number of articles were written and many other poems translated.

I must make it clear that I do not regard Iqbal to be a great religious leader, a doctor of divinity or a man of unquestionable piety and dutifulness to God, nor am I inclined to exaggerate when it comes to the appreciation of his poetry, as the case is with some of his more enthusiastic admirers. I believe that Ḥakim Sanai, Farīduddīn Aṭṭār and Jalāluddīn Rūmī, the Seer, were far ahead of him in these respects. In his lectures on *The Reconstruction of Religious Thought in Islam,* there occur interpretations of certain Islamic concepts with which I do not agree. For example, I do not hold the view that no one had understood and reached the true spirit of Islam better than he had. What I have felt throughout my life is that he was an earnest student of Islamic theology, culture and philosophy who regularly kept in touch with the better known Muslim theologians of his time and sought their advice. His letters to Maulana Anwar Shah Kashmiri, Maulana Syed Sulaiman Nadwi and Maulana Masood Alam Nadwi are illustrative of his humility and keenness for knowledge.

There are certain aspects of Iqbal's unique personality which do not go well with the profundity of his art and learning and the magnificence of his message. Perhaps he did not get an opportunity to overcome these failings. All the same, I believe that Iqbal was a poet whom God had inspired to bring to light certain current truths and doctrines that had not been set forth by any other contemporary poet or thinker. He was a staunch believer in the permanence of the call of Prophet Muḥammad, in the inherent strength and capacity for leadership of the Muslim community and in the insufficiency of modern ideologies and political, social and economic systems. This, I feel, had imparted lucidity and maturity to his thought and led to the growth and development of his individuality. In this respect he was even better than the doctors of Islamic theology who are ignorant of Western thought and culture and who possess little awareness of its real aim and purpose.

I must admit that I find Iqbal a poet of faith, love and sincerity. Whenever I read him I am stirred to the depths of my being. His poetry appeals to my imagination and fills me with an intense warmth and enthusiasm for Islam. This, I think, is the real worth and significance of Iqbal's poetry.

Another incentive to translate Iqbal into Arabic was provided by the humiliating surrender of the Arabs to the materialistic civilisation of the West. I had seen how the Islamic World was standing at the crossroads of ancient and modern Paganism. On one side, it was supposed to choose exaggerated nationalism and, on the other, godless Communism, and the destructive effects of both could be felt in its literature, thought and behaviour. Writers who could understand the significance of the message the Arabs gave to the world and devote their mental capabilities for launching a ceaseless war against the darkness and the intellectual desertion from faith that was strengthening its hold on the educated classes were becoming scarce among the Muslims.

Viewed against this background, the importance of Iqbal became greater. He was born in a newly converted Brahmin family in a country that was under the political and cultural domination of the West. He received education at some of the most outstanding centres of Western learning and yet his faith in the message of Muḥammad ﷺ grew deeper. He came to believe more fervently in the high destiny of the Muslim *Millet*. The justification of Islam and repugnance for Western thought and civilisation became second nature to him. He freely utilised his enormous gifts of heart and intellect in that direction and became a symbol of faith, vision and reflection in Arabia and throughout the Islamic World.

THE GLORY OF IQBAL

I therefore felt that the rendering of Iqbal's poems into Arabic was the best intellectual offering we could make to the rising generations of Islam and the up-and-coming Arab youth. In presenting the book I hope that it will be helpful in breaking the mental apathy and listlessness of Muslims and setting a new trend of thought among them.

CHAPTER ONE

BIOGRAPHICAL SKETCH

Iqbal was born at Sialkot in the Punjab on February 22, 1877. His ancestors, who were Kashmiri Brahmins, had embraced Islam two hundred years earlier. From that time the spirit of piety and fear of God had come to rule over the family. Iqbal's own father was a devout Muslim with a Sufi inclination.

He received his early education in Sialkot. After passing the entrance examination to a local school, he joined the Intermediate College where he was lucky to have Shamsul Ulema Mir Hasan, a great Oriental scholar as his teacher. Mir Hasan had a special aptitude for imparting his own literary taste and distinctive manner to his pupils. Under the influence of this great teacher Iqbal, too, was drawn towards Islamic studies, which he felt had such an effect on him that he was unable to forget them all his life.

Iqbal graduated in English Literature, Philosophy and Arabic from the Government College of Lahore. It was there that he came into contact with Prof. Arnold and Sir Abdul Qadir (whose Urdu magazine, *Makhzan*, was, in those days, one of the most highly regarded periodicals). Iqbal's poem, *Chand* ("Moon") and other early poems appeared in the same journal in 1901 and were acclaimed by critics as the cutting edge of Urdu poetry. After that, it did not take him long to win recognition as a rising star of Urdu literature.

In the meantime, he had completed his M.A. in Philosophy and was appointed Lecturer in History, Philosophy and Political

Science at Oriental College, Lahore. From there, he moved on to Government College to teach Philosophy and English Literature. Wherever Iqbal worked or taught, his versatility and scholarship made a deep impression on those around him.

Iqbal then went to Europe for higher studies in 1905 and stayed there for three years. He took an Honours degree in Philosophy and Economics at Cambridge University and also taught Arabic at the University of London in the absence of Prof. Arnold. From England he went to Munich in Germany to do his Doctorate in Philosophy and then returned to London to qualify for the Bar. He also taught at the London School of Economics and passed the Honours examination in Economics and Political Science. During his stay in Europe Iqbal not only read voraciously but also wrote and gave lectures on Islamic subjects which added to his popularity and fame in literary circles.

The poet returned to Lahore from Europe in 1908. While his ship was passing through the Mediterranean Iqbal burst into tears at the sight of Sicily and said:

> Now weep blood, oh eyes!
> For the tomb of Arab civilisation stands there in sight.

Iqbal had gained all these academic qualifications by the time he was 32 or 33, and from 1908 to 1934 he practised as a lawyer until ill health forced him to give up. However, due to his varied activities he could not give undivided attention to law and he began to devote more time to philosophy and literature than to the legal profession and regularly attended the meetings of Anjuman Himayat-i-Islam regularly at Lahore. It was at one of its annual functions that he read the groundbreaking poem *Shikwa* ("The Complaint") and followed it up, a year later, with *Jawab-i-Shikwa* ("The Answer"). Both of these testified to his genius, made him immensely popular and even became national songs of the *Millet*.

Iqbal wrote two other poems during these days, *Tarana-i-*

Hindi ("The Indian Anthem") and *Tarana-i-Milli* ("The Anthem of the Muslim *Millet"*), which also were very popular and used to be sung as symbols of National or Muslim identity at public meetings.

The Balkan Wars and the Battle of Tripoli in 1910 had a profound effect on Iqbal. He was hurt, agitated and disillusioned and the sentiments of sorrow and indignation that were aroused in him took the form of aversion to Western civilisation and European Imperialism. Anger and frustration forced him to write a number of stirring poems that portrayed the anguish of the Muslims and were severely critical of the West.

The spirit of change and revolt runs through all his poems of that period such as, *Bilad-i-Islamia* ("The Lands of Islam"), *Wataniat* ("Nationalism"), *Muslim, Fatima Bint Abdullah* (who was killed in the siege of Cyrenaica), *Siddiq, Bilal, Hilal-i-'Id* ("The 'Id Crescent"), *Tahzib-i-Hazir* ("Modern Civilisation"), *Din* ("Faith") and *Huzoor-i-Risalat Maab Main* ("In the presence of the Sacred Prophet"). In these poems he bitterly deplores the attitude of Muslim leaders who lay a claim to Islamic leadership and yet are devoid of a genuine spiritual attachment to the blessed Prophet. Iqbal is emphatic in his denunciation of leaders who undertake pilgrimages to the West but are ignorant of the Prophet and are not loyal to him.

> At the Prophet's Mausoleum yesterday a distressed soul was crying,
> Millet's foundations Muslims of India and Egypt are destroying,
> Pilgrims of the shrine of West, however much they claim to be our leaders,
> What can we have to do with them when they are ignorant of thee?

In the dream world, the poet presents himself in the court of the Prophet and when the Prophet asks him what has he brought for him the poet makes this wonderful offering:

> Like perfume you come from the orchards of the earth:
> What bring you then to greet us with, what offering?
> But I have brought this chalice to make my offering,
> It holds a thing not to be found in Paradise.
> See here, Oh, Lord, the honour of thy followers glimmering,
> The martyred blood of Tripoli, Oh Lord, is in this cup

World War I caused great devastation for Muslim countries and Iqbal was profoundly shaken by the tragic events. By this time he had passed through his formative period and had attained maturity as a poet, thinker, and seer. He was able to read the signs of tomorrow in the happenings of today, make predictions, present hard facts and unravel truths through the medium of poetic expression and thus ignite the flame of faith, Selfhood and courage.

His intensity of feeling and enthusiasm were now at their peak. *Khizr-i-Rah* ("The Guide") is the outstanding poem of this period. Each quatrain of it is a masterpiece of artistry, reflection and realism. But *Tulu-i-Islam* ("Dawn of Islam") is the "mansion of *Ghazal*" the like of which can scarcely be found in Islamic literature.

In 1924, Iqbal published his first collection of Urdu verses under the title of *Bang-i-Dara* (*The Caravan Bell*) and since then, it has held a place of honour in both Urdu and world poetry. Its popularity has not waned nor has its effectiveness lost its edge. The period between the publication of *Bang-i-Dara* and Iqbal's death is generally accepted as marking the ripening of his thought and the widening of the frontiers of his learning. In the poems published after 1929, there is a complete balance between poet and seer, and poetry and philosophy. The collections of his Persian poems also appeared during that time.

Iqbal preferred Persian for poetic expression because its circle was wider than that of Urdu and in Muslim India it was the second language. Apart from being the mother tongue in Iran and Afghanistan it was still spoken in larger areas outside India including Central Asia and Turkey. His Persian works, *Asar-i-Khudi* ("Secrets of the Self"), *Rumuz-i-Bekhudi* ("Mysteries of Selflessness"), *Payam-i-Mashriq* ("Message of the East"), *Zabur-i-Ajam* ("The Testament of Iran"), *Javed Nama* ("The Song of Eternity"), *Pas Che Bayad Kard Ali Aqwam-i-Sharq* ("What to do then, O Nations of the East?")[10] and *Musafir* ("Traveller") all belong to the same phase of his life as do his lectures on *The Reconstruction of Religious Thought in Islam* which were extensively appreciated and translated into many languages. Nicholson rendered *Asrar-i -Khudi* into superb English, and academies were set up in Italy and Germany for the study of Iqbal's poetry and philosophy.

In 1927, the poet was elected to the Punjab Legislative Assembly and made important contributions to its deliberations. Then, in 1930, he was elected to preside at the annual session of the Muslim League. It was in his Presidential Address to the Muslim League that Iqbal elaborated the idea of Pakistan for the first time; and in 1930-31, he attended the Round Table Conference which met in London to frame a constitution for India. While in England he was invited by the Governments of France, Spain and Italy to visit those countries and he accepted the offers of hospitality of Spain and Italy and delivered lectures on Islamic art at Madrid. He also went to Cordova and had the distinction of being the first Muslim to offer prayers at its historical Mosque after the exile of the Moors. Memories of the past glory of the Arabs and their 800-year rule over Spain were revived in his mind and his emotions were roused by what he saw. Iqbal has immortalised these moments of bitter grief in a poignant poem which depicts the cultural essence of Islamic Andalusia in words that evoke a great response in the hearts of the readers. It seems that the past had come alive again in the imagination of the poet. The mosque laments over its desolation and pines for the genuflection of the devotees, whilst the sky of Cordova is eager to be filled again with the sound of *Adhān* (the Call to Prayer) since Spain is still shedding tears in the memory of its Islamic splendour.

In Italy, Iqbal was received by Mussolini who had read some of his works and was acquainted with his philosophy. They had a long meeting and talked freely to each other. France, too, was keen that the poet paid a visit to the University of Paris and also went to see the French colonies of North Africa but Iqbal's sense of self-respect did not permit him to accept the invitation. He declined saying that it was too small a price of the destruction of Damascus.

The Universities of Cambridge, Rome and Madrid and the Roman Royal Society organised meetings in his honour and on his way back he also went to Jerusalem to attend the International Conference of Motamar-i-Islami. During the journey he wrote his scintillating poem *Zauq-o-Shauq* ("Ardour and Eagerness").

In 1932, at the invitation of King Nadir Shah, Iqbal visited Afghanistan. He was a member of the delegation of educationists, which also included Sir Ross Masood and Allama Syed Sulaiman Nadwi. The King received the poet with great honour and met him privately, during which time he laid his heart bare and both talked and wept together. At the tombs of Mahmud Ghaznavi and Hakim Sunai, Iqbal was overwhelmed with emotion and his tears again froze into a poem, which he called *Musafir*.

The last phase of Iqbal's life was embittered by constant sickness until his ill-health confined him to bed. However, he was still creatively productive, composing beautiful verses and keeping in touch with current affairs.

> There is a Paradise for the holy men of Haram,[11]
> There is a Paradise for those who dare,
> But tell the Muslims of Hindustan to cheer up,
> There is a Paradise to be doled out in charity too!

A few minutes before his death he recited these touching

lines:
> The departed melody may return or not!
> The zephyr may blow again from Hejaz or not!
> The days of this Faqir have come to an end,
> Another seer may come or not!

Although Iqbal's illness was long, the end was sudden and very peaceful. In the early hours of April 21, 1938, he passed away in the arms of his old and devoted servant, leaving behind a host of mourners all over the Islamic World. There was a faint smile on his lips, which irresistibly reminded one of how he had defined a truthful Muslim.

> I tell you the sign of a true believer [mu'min],
> When death comes there is a smile on his lips

CHAPTER TWO

FORMATIVE FACTORS

Among the characteristics of Iqbal's personality there were also qualities which had little to do with his high academic attainments. The depth of feeling, nobility and sincerity we find in his mental, moral, social and emotional make-up were related to that aspect of life which is known as *belief* and *faith*.

The educational institutions where Iqbal learnt the modern sciences did not alone have a hand in the development of his individuality. He, of course, went to England and Germany for higher studies, and he became the foremost authority on Western philosophy and civilisation in the Muslim World, possessing a deep insight into both ancient and modern branches of learning. However, if Iqbal had remained satisfied with the knowledge gathered from the Western universities, he would not have been the subject of our study today nor would the world of Islamic literature be praising him. The Muslim mind, in that case, would not have opened so spontaneously to him and he would not have risen to such dizzy heights of literary eminence and popularity. No one can hope to attain this position solely on the strength of intellectual accomplishments, for a number of other conditions also have to be fulfilled. Had Iqbal not looked beyond educational institutions he might have become an honoured professor or a well-known writer. He would have won fame as a poet or a scholar of Philosophy, Economics, History or Literature or made a name at the Bar and become a judge of the High Court or secured some other elevated public office. If that had been the case, Iqbal would never have gone the way of all other men of eminence and authority and his reputation would have faded into oblivion with the passage of time. The secret of Iqbal's fire and colour, the real source of the immortality of his message, was embedded far away from the traditional centre of learning. Rather, it lay in an "institution" which is absolutely unique, and it was here that Iqbal learnt what he tried to convey through the magic of his poems all his life.

You will naturally be anxious to know what this "institution" was that gave rise to a superb poet like him. What subjects are taught there? How do they teach people and who are its teachers? Surely, the teaching staff of an institution that can produce a poet of Iqbal's calibre must be of a very high order. I am convinced that once you come to know of it you will try to gain admission into it and commit your training to the care of its wonderful guides and teachers.

No one who received education in it was unsuccessful and no one who passes out of it can ever be lost. It is an "institution" from which only leaders of thought, doctors of law and divinity, initiators of branches of learning and reformers and renovators emerge. What they write is prescribed for study in schools and colleges, students burn midnight oil over their works and commentaries are written on them. Their views are widely discussed and scholars examine theories put forward by them in detail. In this "institution" history is made, not taught. Here ideas and opinions are formulated, not analysed and truths are produced, not sought and studied. It is the inner "school," which is born with everyone and remains with him till death. It is the "institution" of the heart; the "seminary" of conscience, where Divine education is imparted and spiritual development takes place.

Like many other naturally gifted men, Iqbal completed his education at this marvellous "institution." His character and personality, knowledge and learning, morality and disposition owed their development to the "seminary" of the heart. As a study of his works will confirm, the internal school had a greater hand in the engendering of warmth, sincerity and depth of feeling in his life than the external school. Iqbal's personality would never have been so fascinating and his intuition so keen had he not received education in it. Nor would have his message become the living flame it was. In his poems he frequently alluded to teachers, mentors and benefactors of this "seminary" and expressed his deepest gratitude to them.

All the five fundamental elements, which nurtured and moulded Iqbal's individuality and fulfilled it, belonged to this inner school. Firstly, there was the attribute of belief and faith. It was Iqbal's chief instructor and the main source of his vitality and wisdom. However, Iqbal's faith did not consist of a soulless dogma or a mechanical formula of affirmation. Rather, his entire existence consisted of belief and love and his ideas and emotions, likes and dislikes and friendship and enmity were governed by it. That is why Iqbal believed so strongly in Islam and his love and devotion for the Holy Prophet was limitless. For him Islam was an eternal, everlasting religion outside of which mankind could not work out its destiny. The sacred Prophet was the guide and the leader and master of one and all.

> The Pathfinder, last Messenger of God, master of all,
> Who on the road-dust bestowed the splendour of Sinai?

Iqbal was not attracted to the glitter of the modern materialistic civilisation even though he had spent many years in the West. This was due to his deep religious devotion, love for the Prophet and immense spiritual attachment to him.

> The glare of Frankish[12] SCIENCE COULD NOT CONFUSE MY VISION,
> For the dust of Madinah and Najaf is the collyrium of my eyes.
> What a curse modern learning is, I know,

Since I was cast in its fire like Khalīl.[13]
The Pharaohs plotted, and yet plot against me, what harm?
In my sleeve I possess the luminous hand of Moses.
What wonder if the Plaedias or the high moon fall my prey,
For I have bound my head to the Prophet's saddle bow.

In *Asrar-i-Khudi* Iqbal also speaks of the intensity of his devotion and loyalty to the Prophet while discussing the basic constituents of the Muslim *Millet,* and the foundations upon which it is built. His poetic instinct is aroused to its peak when he talks about the sacred Prophet, and verses begin to flow freely and smoothly from his pen. We will refer to the lines given below to illustrate our point.

In the Muslim's heart is the name of Muḥammad,
All our glory is from the name of Muḥammad.
He slept on a mat of rushes,
But the crown of Chosroes was under his followers' feet.
He chose the nightly solitude of Mount Ḥirā',
And he founded a nation, laws and government.
He passed many a night with sleepless eyes,
In order that the *Millet* might sleep on Chosroes' throne.
In the hour of battle, iron was melted by the flash of his sword,
In the hour of prayer, tears fell like rain from his eyes.
When he prayed for Divine help, his sword answered "Amen,"
And extirpated the race of kings.
He instituted a new Law in the world,
He brought the empire of antiquity to an end.
With the key of religion he opened the door of this world,
The womb of the world never bore his like,
In his sight high and low were one,
He sat with his slave at one table.
The daughter of the chieftain of Tai was taken prisoner in battle,
And brought into that exalted presence;
Her feet in chains, her face unveiled,
And her neck bowed with shame.

> When the Prophet saw that the poor girl had no veil,
> He covered her face with his own mantle.
> He opened the gates of mercy to his enemies,
> He gave to Makkah the message: "There's no blame on you today."
> We who know not the prison walls of country,
> Resemble sight, which is one though it is the light of two eyes.
> We belong to Arabia and China and Persia,
> Yet are the dew of one smiling dawn.
> We are all under the spell of the eye of the cupbearer of Madinah,
> We are united as wine and cup.
> He burnt clean the distinctions of birth and race,
> His fire consumed this trash and rubble.
> The song of love for him fills my silent reed,
> A hundred notes throb in my bosom.
> What to speak of the praise I sing of him,
> Even the block of dry wood wept at parting from him.[14]
> The Muslim's being is where he manifests his glory,
> Many a Sinai springs from the dust of his path.

Iqbal's passionate devotion to the sacred Prophet grew with the passage of time, and during the last phase of his life if the name of the Prophet was mentioned in his presence or someone began to talk about the blessed cities of Makkah and Madinah he became restless and could not control his tears. It was this feeling of spiritual attachment that inspired him to compose verses of unmatched beauty and excellence. For instance, he begs God in these words:

> Disgrace me not before the Master,
> Call me to account away from his sight.

How superbly symbolic of love and loyalty these lines are! The warmth, fervour, anguish and distress one experience in Iqbal's poems have their roots in the perfection of faith and love. Whether it is a moving verse or a profound idea or any other form of high artistic or intellectual ability, it is essentially the gift of faith and love; and whatever evidence of the glory and greatness of man is found in history it has its origin in the two basic attributes of the heart. A person who is devoid of these fundamental qualities is merely flesh. A community that cannot lay claim to one's inner wealth of faith and love is no more than a herd of cattle. The same is true of poetry as well. A poet who is not inspired by faith and love can, at best, be only a rhymester. He may make rhymes but cannot write living poetry, and his book becomes a mere collection of pages. In the same way, if worship is not endowed with the spirit of faith and love, it becomes a lifeless ritual. Life itself becomes like death if it fails to fulfil this condition. When the spirits are dejected, existence, poetry and literature become worthless. When things come to such a point, true faith and sincere love come to the rescue by reviving the nobler feelings and reactivating religious, moral, and artistic sensitivity. Elegant, moving, heart-warming verses then become a show of super human courage and endurance and attain immortality. If love even penetrates into clay, water or stone it invests it with eternity as we find in the case of the Taj Mahal, Qasr-e-Azhar and the Mosque of Cordova.

> Works of creation are incomplete without the heart's warm blood,
> Music an immature frenzy, without the heart's warm blood.

It is wrong to imagine that men of letters excel one another merely on the strength of their intellect and scholarship, that poets owe their successes solely to natural aptitude and choice of words or that the eminence of a leader or reformer is related wholly to his political acumen, wisdom and eloquence. Their greatness stems primarily from the spirit of love and dedication without which no one's work can become the passion of his life or spread through his being, taking command of his heart, will and action. When these attributes are present in the identity of a poet, writer or reformer he becomes so involved in his mission that when he speaks he speaks with its tongue and when he writes he writes with its pen. The purpose, in short, becomes his destiny, engulfing his whole being.

The worst of the gifts of modern civilisation is the materialism that, in its turn, breeds commercialism and self-indulgence. It is basically the outcome of the current system of education, which is totally unrelated to man's inner needs. Thus, our rising generations are becoming bankrupt from within and are heading blindly towards ruin and destruction. Their hearts contain neither the warmth of faith nor the restlessness of love and the joy of conviction, and the modern world has turned out to be a dull, drab and dreary affair in which there is neither life nor awareness, neither the sensation of joy nor the consciousness of sorrow.

Iqbal's poetry is strikingly different from that of other celebrated poets. It never fails to evoke warmth and yearning and pain and restlessness within us. It bursts upon us and melts the chains of materialism whilst doing away with perverse social and moral standards. It reveals how strong the faith of the poet is.

Another thing which moulded Iqbal's character was what is present today in every Muslim home, although, many Muslims have ceased to derive light and wisdom from it. I mean the Holy Quran, which had exerted a tremendous influence on the life and philosophy of Iqbal. He had not been impressed so deeply by anyone nor moved so powerfully be any other book than the Quran. Since the faith of Iqbal was that of a "convert" and he had not inherited it from family there was in him a far greater attachment to the Quran and keenness to study it carefully than the so-called lineal Muslims customarily have. Iqbal's recitation of the Quran was not like that of any other Muslim. The poet has said himself that he used to recite the Quran daily after the Dawn Prayer. Whenever his father saw him reading it he would ask, "What are you doing?" he would reply, "I am reciting the Quran." After some time Iqbal plucked up the courage to say to his father, "You ask me the same question every day and I give the same reply, and then you go away." Iqbal's father then remarked, "I want to tell you that you should recite the Quran as if it was being revealed to you there and then." Consequently, Iqbal made it a point to read the Quran in such a way that it was as if it was really being sent down to him at that very moment. He also explained the significance of it in one of his verses:

> Unless the Book descends upon your spirit,
> no interpreter, neither Rāzī[15]
> nor he who wrote "The Key,"[16]
> shall unravel the knot for you.

Iqbal devoted his whole life to the study of the Quran. He read the Quran, thought the Quran and spoke the Quran. It was his favourite Book, which opened new vistas of knowledge for him and gave him fresh awareness and strength. As his study of the Quran progressed, his mind attained greater loftiness and his faith developed further mellowness since it was an eternal Book, revealing transcendental truths and leading on to everlasting happiness. It is the master key, which can open all the doors of human existence. It is a complete, well-defined and all-embracing programme for life and a guide in times of darkness.

The third factor was the realisation of the "Self" or Ego. Iqbal has laid the greatest emphasis on the cultivation and growth of Selfhood. He believed that the true development of the personality could not take place without self-realisation. Unless the evolution of the Ego took place, life must remain an empty dream, devoid of yearning, sincerity, ecstasy and intoxication.

> Delve deep into your buried Self, and find the clue to life,
> If you cannot be mine then be not, but be your own,
> World of soul-world of fire, ecstasy and longing,
> World of body-a world of gain, fraud and cunning;
> The treasure of the spirit once gained is never lost again,
> The treasure of the body is a shadow—wealth comes and goes,
> In the world of soul I have found no Frankish rule,

In that world no Sheikh or Brahmin I have seen;
This saying of the Qalandar[17] poured shame and shame on me,
When you kneel to another's might neither body nor soul is your own.

Besides thought content, the sound-pattern and underlying sincerity of these verses are so enchanting that one feels like reading them again and again. Iqbal placed a great value on the disciplining of Selfhood and the cultivation of the Ego and according to him, self-development taught mankind the secrets of power and rule. Whether Attār or Rūmī, Rāzī or Ghazālī, no one could achieve anything without it. It was the realisation of self-development that led Iqbal to prefer death to the materialistic and atheistic civilisation. Only he who had attained the goal of self-realisation could have the courage to proclaim:

The code of men of courage is truth and fearlessness,
God's lions know not the cunning of a fox.

Iqbal's conception of Selfhood had become the essence of his being. His own existence was a glowing example of his idea of self-realisation. His life is a perfect example of self-dignity, self-reliance and self-development. In the verses reproduced below he asks of others what he practised himself till death.

If the kings know not their Sustainer they are beggars,
And if the beggars do they are Darius and Jamshed,
Freedom of the heart is sovereignty; stomach is death,
The choice is yours; heart or stomach?

It was the awareness of Self that protected Iqbal against intellectual unpredictability and literary waywardness which often caused our poets and writers to try to cover every aspect of human existence, no matter whether it went well with their mental and moral outlook or not. They consequently remain strangers to themselves throughout their lives and end up frustrated. Iqbal, however, was a grand exception. He knew himself thoroughly from day one and employed his gifts of heart and intellect to shake the Muslims out of their stupor and stir the spark of faith that was lying dormant in them. He used his poetical ability to instil the spirit of freedom, strength and leadership in them.

Iqbal was a born poet and even if he had tried to shun poetry he would not have succeeded. His poetry was a symbol of the bleeding heart, of ardency, enthusiasm, profoundness and sensitive imagery and he enjoyed a complete command over the art of verse making. His contemporaries not only acknowledged his genius and admired the wonderful quality of his verses but were also impressed by the originality of his thought and technique. He coined new similes and metaphors and introduced new symbols, drawing liberally upon English, German and Persian literature to enrich his art. It was not that there were no outstanding poets in India during the days of Iqbal, but what distinguished Iqbal from them were his poetic majesty, imaginative vivacity and intellectual artistry, and, to crown it all, there was his passionate devotion to Islam.

Iqbal was not a national poet. His poetic genius was not restricted by the frontiers of race or geography. He was not one of the romantic poets who are inspired only by luxuriousness and lovers. His poetry was not altogether soaked in wisdom and philosophy. The call of Islam and the message of the Quran inspired him and he used his poetic ability to preach and propagate the beliefs that were dearest to his heart. There is no doubt that he awakened people from their deep sleep and rekindled the flame of faith in them. Iqbal had discovered himself and made a correct judgement of his potentialities and put them to proper use.

The fourth element, which went in the making of Iqbal's personality and endowing his poetry with sublimity, forcefulness and vitality, had nothing to do with study and scholarship. It was the sigh of the early hours of the morning. When the world was asleep Iqbal used to get up and devote himself to lamentation and prayer. It energised his mind and gave a new light and joy to his soul. Having thus re-equipped himself, mentally and spiritually, before the sun had risen he would offer unparalleled verses to the world.

In Iqbal's view early morning devotions were a most precious part of life, which even the greatest of scholars, ascetics and philosophers, could not afford to neglect.

> Aṭṭār or Rūmī, Rāzī or Ghazālī-whoever may be,
> Nothing is attained without the pre-dawn wail.

Iqbal always left his bed very early whether he was at home or on a journey.

> Sharp as a sword through the wintry air of Europe,
> I gave up not the habit of early rising even there.

He begged to God to take back from him whatever he pleased but not the joy of wailing at dawn.

> Deprive me not of the joy of pre-dawn sigh,
> Do not temper the indifference of thy glance with mercy.

Iqbal wished to see his wailing and lamentation, agony and restlessness, in the young Muslims and prayed for the torment of his heart and his love and vision to be passed on to them.

> Bestow on the youth the suffering of the heart,
> Grant to it my love and vision!

In another poem he says:

> Grant the youth my morning wail!
> To the eaglets give again feathers and wings!
> O Lord! I have but one wish-
> Give to all and sundry the gift of my foresight!

The wish and prayer of Iqbal did not go unnoticed for today, in the Muslim World, a new generation is emerging who are true to Islamic thought and understanding.

The fifth and the last factor was the *Mathnawi-i-Ma'nawi* of Maulana Jalāluddīn Rūmī. Intuitive experience and spiritual animation inspired this immortal Persian poem of unequalled worth. At the time of Maulana Rūmī, Greek philosophy had become so predominant in the Muslim World that it was extremely difficult to open a new avenue of thought. Distressed at this sad state of affairs the Maulana began to write his *Mathnawi* which abounds with literary sublimity, originality of meaning, wise parables, and wise advice. Many people have been influenced by it and their mental and spiritual attitude has been transformed. It is a unique work of its kind in Islamic and world literature. When Iqbal came into contact with the godless and vulgar materialistic doctrines of the West the conflict between the matter and spirit within him reached the climax he turned to the *Mathnawi* for assistance. It proved extremely helpful to him in the hour of inner confusion and perplexity and he began to regard the Sage of Rūmī an ideal mentor. He declared that the solution to the confusion of wisdom and intellect, which had been made more complicated by Western materialism, lay in the warmth generated by the Flame of Rūmī. It was because of the Maulana's *Mathnawi* that his own vision had been illuminated, and awareness had come to him.

> In the heart of the Fire of Rūmī is your remedy,
> On your intellect the Franks have cast their spell,
> My eye is illuminated by his grace,
> By his munificence Jaihun[18] is contained in my ewer.

Time and again Iqbal lets us know how deep his love and regard for the Maulana whom he fondly calls the Sage of Rūmī really is,

> The Sage of Rūmī, an enlightened mentor,
> Leader of the caravan of love and ecstasy.
> In the company of the Sage of Rūmī have I learnt,
> One fearless heart is worth a thousand wise heads muffled in a sack.

In the present age of crude materialism and soulless technology Iqbal awaits the appearance of another Rūmī. He believes that the problem of materialism can be removed only by love for which the Flame of Rūmī is needed once again.

> From the flowerbeds of *ʿAjam*[19] no new Rūmī arose,
> Though the soil and water of Iran is the same, Oh Saqi,[20] and

so is of Tabrez.

But Iqbal is not disheartened.

> Of his desolate sowing-field Iqbal shall not despair,
> A little rain and the soil is most fertile, oh Saqi!

These were the five factors that shaped Iqbal's personality and caused its development. All of them were the outcome of the instruction he received at the 'peerless' institution which gave him a strong faith, a balanced mind and a majestic ideal and thus made him what he was.

CHAPTER THREE

WESTERN CIVILISATION

At the end of the 19TH century Muslim young men began to be attracted by Western education and many joined the universities founded by the British rulers. One of the advantages of it was that the fear of the ruling nation was dispelled from their hearts and cultural contacts with it were established. Muslims overcame their diffidence and confidently set out on the path of higher education. Under the supervision of Western teachers they got the opportunity of seeing the West from close quarters and evaluating the fundamental characteristics of its civilisation.

Through Western philosophy and literature, the Muslims became acquainted with the mysteries of the Occident and learnt to understand its intrinsically materialistic disposition and the arrogant nationalism underlying its collective consciousness. The other weaker aspects of the Western way of life and the signs of its inner bankruptcy and spiritual degeneration were also revealed to them. The outcome of this was that they realised how the finer qualities of human mind and character were not only lacking in it but also being deliberately neglected by its leaders. All the degenerate attributes, which had also been present from the beginning as part of its nature, were now evident to them. Intellectual awakening and the resultant desire for action could not, however, be produced without a prolonged stay in Europe. A fearless and strong mind was needed along with an intimate knowledge of Western philosophy and civilisation to bring about the reaction.

When the hidden spark of faith was at last stirred, the modern educated Muslims were seized with a strong sense of disappointment in respect of the West and a bold and healthy spirit of criticism was engendered in them, which nevertheless was basically fair, logical and objective.

Iqbal was foremost among the intellectual critics of the West. It can perhaps be said that the modern educated Muslim classes have not produced a greater man of vision than him during the last hundred years. He was the most accomplished thinker of the East. Among the Oriental scholars, no one can be said to have possessed the depth of Iqbal's understanding of the West and the courage and resoluteness of his judgement.

Iqbal had clearly understood the inherent weaknesses of Western thought and culture, its faulty and deficient features and the elemental perversity of its design. He had realised how disdainfully the Western mind dealt with transcendental truths and felt that its depravity was chiefly the outcome of the uncleanness of the soul of the civilisation it represented. He says:

> Civilisation of the West is perversion of heart and mind,
> Since its soul could not remain unpolluted.
> When the soul loses its purity everything goes,
> Cleanliness of conscience, loftiness of mind, refinement of taste.

In spite of the mighty empires the West had built and the glamour and enlightenment that were associated with it, the Western society was seething with discontent.

> This unbounded luxury, this government, this trade,
> But the heart in the unilluminated breast unblest with peace;
> Dark is the Frankish country with the smoke of its machines,
> This "Valley of blessedness and hope" not worthy of Divine Splendour.
> A civilisation sick before its prime, at its last gasp,
> The Jews likely to be the sole trustees of Christendom.

Iqbal refers time after time to the godless character of the

Western philosophy of life whose foundation is laid on the intolerance of religion and ethics and the favourite pastime of which, during all the stages of history, has been the carving of new images. In the *Mathnawi, Pas Che Bayed Kard*, he says that the wicked civilisation had been continually at war with men of Truth and has spread its mischief by installing the idols of *Lāt* and *'Uzza*[21] in the sacred enclosure of the House of Ka'ba. The heart becomes dark and the soul is killed because of its sorcery. It is the robber that strikes in broad daylight and leaves a man a pauper morally, mentally and spiritually.

> Of this civilisation of ungodliness beware!
> At war which is with men of truth;
> The mischief-monger nothing but mischief breeds,
> In the Ḥaram[22] it reinstalls the idols of Lāt and 'Uzza.
> By its sorcery the eye of the heart is sightless,
> The soul thirsty with its barrenness;
> The joy of eagerness it kills in the heart,
> Nay, the heart itself it destroys.
> The depravations of the old thief are for all to see,
> Even the tulip cries, "What have they done to my scar?"

Annihilation of man is the profession of this civilisation and trade and commerce is its sole aim and occupation. As long as it is predominant in the world there will be no peace amongst men, no selfless love and no sincerity.

> Europe, alas, is ignorant of this state,
> With the light of Allah its eye does not see.
> Nor between the allowed and the prohibited it makes a distinction,
> Its wisdom is immature and mission incomplete.
> One sows the seeds; another reaps the harvest;
> In snatching bread from the weak its wisdom lies,
> And in taking away from his brother's frame.

The target of modern Civilisation is man himself who is the source of its energy and animation and the instrument of its commerce and industry. The mounting expenditures and the rising cost of living are the creations of Jewish cunning, which have robbed mankind of the light of faith. Religion, culture and wisdom must remain a dream until the prevalent outlook on life is radically altered.

> Annihilation of man is the business of modern civilisation,
> And the cloak it uses is trade.
> Thanks to the banks, these products of Jewish ingenuity,
> The light of Truth from man has departed.
> Till this system from the world is uprooted,
> Religion, wisdom and culture must remain a dream.
> Although young, the Western Civilisation is already ready to disintegrate.
> A Civilisation sick before its prime, at its last gasp,
> The Jews are likely to be the sole trustees of Christendom.

If it does not die a natural death it will kill itself as it has been built on weak and instable foundations that are unable to withstand the onslaught of time. The technological advancement of the West is a threat to itself and to the world as a whole.

> The arrant intellect that laid bare the treasures of nature,
> In its own nest is threatened by the lightning it released.

The world of profit, trade, deceit and depravity is crumbling fast and a new world is struggling to take its place.

> But now a new world is born, the old world is dying,
> The world the dice-throwers of Europe have made a gambling den.

The civilisation of the West is not lacking in lustre and the flame of life burns brightly in it but it does not possess a Moses to whom Divine inspiration may have come and a *Khalīl*[23] who can break the idols.

In it, the intellect thrives and flourishes but a corresponding withering away of love and other human emotions is taking place. Even the so-called revolutionaries of the modern world do not have the courage to shake off the chains of convention and narrow-mindedness. Their progressive outlook remains a slave to custom and usage.

> Remember the days I was in the tavern of the West,
> The cups of which glittered even more than the mirror of Alexander,
> To wine the intoxicated eyes of bartender, the creator,
> The glance of the cupbearer to wine-drinkers, the Prophet.
> Without a Kalim whose splendour is, without a Khali! whose fire,
> Reckless intellect the enemy of love's fortune.
> Its atmosphere is devoid of the heat of the impatient sigh,
> And patrons without the stumble of an intoxicated soul.

> Mankind is sick at heart because of Franks,
> And life in perpetual turmoil.
> To its own sword Europe has fallen a victim,
> Under the sky the cult of atheism it founded.
> Man's troubles all emanate from it,
> Of humanity's hidden sorrow it is the cause.
> Man is mere water and clay in its sight,
> And life's caravan without a destination.

In the West there is apparently a profusion of the light of knowledge and science, but, in fact, this "Ocean of Darkness" is without the "Fount of Life." Typical of the materialistic civilisation, the buildings of the banks are far superior to those of the Churches, and the whole notion of trade is based upon the profit of one man and the death of millions. Politics and Government and knowledge and learning of which the West is excessively proud are meaningless concepts behind which there is no reality. The achievements of the people who are devoid of Divine grace do not extend beyond the domain of technology and progress. In a civilisation dominated by machines and characterised by exclusive preoccupation with material profit, death of the heart, destruction of mutual understanding and extinction of human glory are certain.

> Though Europe is radiant with the light of knowledge,
> The "Ocean of Darkness" is barren of the "Fount of Life."

> In splendour, in seduction and in grace,
> The buildings of banks outsoar the Houses of God.
> In appearance, it is trade, in reality gambling,
> Profit for one, for thousands sudden death.
> Science, Philosophy, College, Constitution,
> Preach man's equality and suck men's blood.
> Want and unemployment, lewdness and intoxication,
> Are these mean triumphs of the Occident?
> A nation unblessed by Divine Light,
> Steam and electricity bound its works.

A more penetrating study of the Western Civilisation is found in Iqbal's lectures on *The Reconstruction of Religious Thought in Islam*. Dwelling upon the materialistic foundations of the Western cultural and intellectual design and the host of problems it has succeeded in creating for mankind in the different spheres of individual and collective existence Iqbal remarks:

> Wholly shadowed by the results of his intellectual activity, the modern man has ceased to live soulfully, i.e., from within. In the domain of thought, he is living in open conflict with himself and in the domain of political life, he is living in open conflict with others. He finds himself unable to control his ruthless egoism and his infinite gold-hunger, which are gradually killing the entire higher striving and bringing nothing but life-weariness. Absorbed in the "fact," that is to say, the optically present source of sensation, he is entirely cut off from the unplumbed depths of his own being. In the wake of his systematic materialism has at last come that paralysis of energy which Huxley apprehended and deplored....Modern atheistic socialism, which possesses all the fervour of a new religion, has a broader outlook; but having received its philosophical basis from the left-wing Hegelians it rises in revolt against the very source which could have given it strength and purpose. Both nationalism and atheistic socialism, at least at the present state of human adjustments, must draw upon the psychological forces of hate, suspicion and close up his hidden sources of spiritual energy. Neither the technique of medieval mysticism nor nationalism nor atheistic socialism can cure the ills of despairing

humanity....It is only by rising to a fresh vision of his origin and future, his whence and whither, that man will eventually triumph over a society motivated by an inhuman competition, and a civilisation which has lost its spiritual unity by its inner conflict of spiritual and religious values!

Western society is founded upon competition and class-conflict and derives its energy and dynamism from these. The division between political and religious values and the differentiation between matter and spirit has destroyed its organic unity. Iqbal regards Capitalism and Communism to be the two branches of the same tree of materialism. The former is Western in its origin and the other Eastern but they both join one another where the materialistic interpretation of reality and the limitation of humanity are concerned. Depicting in *Javed Nama,* in an imaginary meeting with Jamāluddīn Afghānī, Iqbal expresses the view through him that the West, after depriving itself of spiritual values and transcendental truths, is trying to seek the soul, though the soul has nothing to do with the physical structure of life and energy. Communism is not capable of looking beyond this either and its ideal of human brotherhood cannot be attained through economic equality alone. For it, true love, high ethical standards and spiritual orientation are necessary.

> The Westerners have lost the vision of heaven,
> They go hunting for the pure spirit in the body,
> The pure soul takes not colour and scent from the body,
> And Communism has nothing to do save with the body.
> The religion of that Apostle who knew not truth,
> Is founded upon equality of the belly;
> The abode of fraternity being in the heart,
> Its roots are in the heart, not in water and clay.

In the same way, there is little to choose between Communism and Imperialism when it comes to greed, disorder, godlessness and exploitation. If life in Communism is production, in Imperialism it is taxation. Between the two, the poor and helpless man is being ground down. Communism is the enemy of religion, morality, art and learning, while Imperialism is thirsting for the blood of the masses which it sucks from the rich and the poor alike. Both of these systems are motivated by materialism and on the surface they may appear fresh and radiant, but are inwardly dark and corrupt.

> The soul of both of them is impatient and restless,
> Both of them know not God, and deceive mankind.
> One lives by production, the other by taxation,
> And man is a glass caught between the two stones.
> The one puts to rout, science, religion and art,
> The other robs the body of soul, the hand of bread.
> I have perceived both drowned in water and clay,
> Both bodily burnished, but utterly dark of heart.
> Life means a passionate burning, an urge to make,
> To cast in the dead clay the seed of a heart.

Iqbal is convinced that the Western Civilisation cannot save the Islamic World. It can neither solve its problems nor give it a new lease of life. He asks how a civilisation, which is itself in the throes of death, can revive and resuscitate others?

> Even the naked truth they cannot see,
> Whose vision servility has blurred,
> How can Iran, Arabia suck new life,
> From the West which itself is at grave's edge?

The West has always looked down upon the East and has returned its kindness with ingratitude and good with evil. Syria gave Christ to the West who preached piety, righteousness, compassion and kindness as well as clemency and forgiveness but the West rewarded it with oppression, lewdness, intemperance and gambling.

> To the Franks the dust of Syria gave,
> The Apostle of chastity, compassion, love.
> The Franks to Syria, in return, have sent,
> Wine, gambling and prostitution.

Iqbal is mistrustful of Modernism, or rather, of Westernisation in the East. He fears that their progressivism is merely a pretext for wholesale surrender to the Western philosophy of life.

> The cry of Modernisation is East, I fear,
> Is but pretence for imitation of the West.

Deploring the spiritual and intellectual poverty of the advocates of reform and Westernisation he observes:

> Of thy conjouror-cupbeareres I have despaired,
> Who in the assembly of the East have brought an empty ewer.
> What new lightning can there be in these clouds,
> When even the old lightning they possess no more?

Imitation of other people's cultural and intellectual attitudes, customs and practices is unacceptable to Iqbal. It is shameful, he says, for any community to do so, to speak nothing of the imitation of the one which has been raised up for the leadership of the world.

> Who in the world of creation is a creative man,
> Round him Time does not cease to circumambulate.
> Destroy not the worth of your Ego by imitation,
> Protect it zealously for this pearl is unique.
> Let that community go ahead with the cult of Modernism,
> For which the nightly pleasures are ambition's end.
> The cry of Modernisation in the East, I fear,
> Is but pretence for the imitation of the West.

The Islamic countries that have degraded themselves to the position of being the worthless disciples and imitators of the West, while, in fact, they were intended to be guides and leaders of mankind have been severely taken to task by Iqbal. Speaking of the Turks he observes more in sorrow than in anger that:

> Who could as leaders of their Age function,
> The dotards, alas, have become its slaves.

In *Javed Nama* Iqbal puts the following verses in the mouth of Sa'eed Halim Pasha to describe the shallowness and superficiality of the Turkish Revolution and the intellectual sterility and imitativeness of its main architect, Mustafa Kamal.

> Mustafa Kamal, who sang of a great renewal,
> Said the old image must be cleansed and polished.
> Yet the vitality of the Kaʿba cannot be made new,
> If new Lāt and Manāt from the West are imported.
> No, the Turks have no new melody in their lute,
> What they call new is only the old tune of Europe.
> No new breath has entered into their breast,
> No design of a new world is in their mind.
> Turkey perforce goes along with the existing world,
> Melted like wax in the flame of the world we know.

The Western educational system is a slow but unrelenting genocide practised on the people of the East by the rulers of the West. In the place of the old and condemned method of physical extermination, the Western educationists have preferred the technique of casting a whole generation into their mould and, with this end, intellectual factories are being set up, from place to place, under the names of schools and colleges. The following verses from *Akbar Allahabadi* throw some light on the plan.

> Pharaoh would not have earned notoriety for infanticide,
> Had the idea of founding a college crossed his mind.

> Rulers of the East break the enemy's head,
> Those of West alter his nature.

Iqbal, with a first-hand experience of the Western educational system, expresses the same idea with greater seriousness and solidity. He says:

> Be not complacent about the education you receive,
> Through it the soul of a nation they can kill.

Iqbal denounces the Western educational system as a conspiracy against religion and morality.

> Treat its Ego with the acid of education,
> When it softens, give it the shape you please.
> More efficacious than elixir this acid is,
> A mountain of gold it reduces to dust.

Iqbal was one of the very few fortunate young men who not

only made it back safely from his encounter with Western education but also brought with him some idea of the need for the restoration of faith in the Muslims and in the eternity and comprehensiveness of the message of Islam.

Though it is difficult to say that Iqbal remained completely unaffected by Western philosophy and education or that his religious understanding wholly conformed to the teachings of the Book (the Holy Quran) and the *Sunnah*, the "Fire of Namrud" had definitely failed to destroy his Islamic individuality as the case was with thousands of his contemporaries.

> The spell of modern education I broke,
> I picked the grain, left the net alone,
> God knows how in the manner of Ibrāhīm,
> I sat in its fire easy in mind.

CHAPTER FOUR

MODERN EDUCATION

Iqbal discovered a number of weaknesses in the modern education system. He frankly and constructively criticised its faults and inadequacies, bringing them into the notice of experts in educational methods.

When Iqbal speaks of "schools," "seminaries" and "students" he generally means the Western or Westernised institutions of education and their scholars. According to him, the present system of education is a curse to the rising generations and is doing more harm than good. He is displeased both with the *Madrassa* (seminary) and *Khanqah* (sufi-lodge) where neither the zest for life is witnessed nor are the ardour of love, knowledge or idealism fostered.

> I rose downhearted from *Madrassa* and *Khanqah* where,
> Neither life is promoted nor love nor knowledge nor vision.

He also frowns upon the bankruptcy of the schools and the soulnessness of the monasteries.

> The scholars of *Madrassa* ignorant and listless.
> The hermits of *Khanqah* shallow and unambitious

Iqbal feels that modern education is an evil because it neglects both the mental, moral and spiritual development of the younger generations. The result is that a crisis of character has overtaken the youth. Having been brought up in this way it is finding it hard to adjust itself to the environment and to the hard realities of the surrounding world. If the younger men everywhere are inclined to be wayward and restless it is due to the emotional imbalance that has been created in them through education. A deep conflict has been caused between their inner and outer selves, their mind and body, and knowledge and belief. They have developed a split personality.

The intellect of today's young Muslims is radiant but dark. Its spiritual degeneration has been taking place side-by-side with mental development. Iqbal knows the younger generation intimately, and, therefore, what he says about them and the way he judges them is realistic. He complains that they are lacking faith and love even though outwardly they present a picture of brightness and vitality. They are luminous, yet blind when it comes to discernment and perception. Hesitation, incertitude and despondency are the characteristic traits of its personality and disappointment is its future. The young men are not young; they are living corpses. They deny their own identity but are ever willing to put their faith in others. Aliens and strangers are building the church and temple out of the Islamic heaven and the Muslim youth has grown indolent, lazy and ease loving. It is so apathetic and insipid that it has lost touch with ambition. The modern educational system has blunted its soul and made it virtually lifeless.

Among the Muslim young men, the unawareness of the Self and indifference towards their destiny are widespread. Under the influence of the Western civilisation the Muslim youth is ready to barter away its soul for a few crumbs of bread and they feel no guilt at borrowing idols from the West. The mentors of the rising generations, being themselves ignorant of their true worth, take little interest in teaching them the secrets of greatness and nobility. They are Muslims, yet are unaware of the joy of death and unacquainted with the power of *Tawḥīd* (the doctrine of Monotheism). As Iqbal says, the "sons of *Ḥaram*" are not averse to making a pilgrimage to the "street of infamy" and prostrating themselves at the "feet of the mistress"

Modern Education

The idols of modern days carved in the school,
Bear neither the touch of Āzar[24] nor posses charm
My complaint against mentors of the school is this:
To eaglets they impart the lesson of earthliness.
People of the seminary have strangled thee,
Wherefrom the sound of *Lā Ilāha Illa'Allāh*[25] can come?
Does the Madrassa possess the beauty of thought?
Is the joy of mystery in the Khanqah present?
From the wine of faith is the warmth of life,
Grant this liquid fire, Oh Lord, to seminary too.
Is this the whole fortune of the modern world—
Luminous mind, gloomy heart, arrant eye?
Ah I the hot-blooded youth of the school—
Hapless victim of the witchery of the West.
The young are thirsty; their cup is empty,
Their visages are polished souls dark, intellects bright.
Devoid of vision, bereft of faith, shorn of hope,
Nothing in the world did his eye perceive.
The worthless men, untrue to themselves, servile to others,
The architect of the temple, from their clay had laid the bricks

Nevertheless, Iqbal is not dismayed. He has faith in the growing generations and his poems are full of hope and encouragement for the youth.

I am in love with the young men who,
Cast their noose on the stars.
Grant the youth my morning wail!
To the eaglets give again feathers and wings!
O Lord! I have but one wish-
Give to all and sundry the gift of my foresight!

A glimpse of his hopes and expectations can be seen in *Khitab Ba Jawanan-i-Islam* ("An Address to the Young Men of Islam") and some other poems. His message to the scholars of Muslim University, Aligarh, for instance, contains the following verse:

From the passion of *Ḥaram* is the glory of Arabia,
Its place is different, its law unique.

The poem, *Ek Naujawan ke Nam* ("To a Young Man") is also

richly representative of his ideas and feelings.

> Your sofas are from Europe, your fine carpets from Iran;
> My eyes weep blood when I see such pampered ways among young men!
> For what are rank and office, what even the pomp of Chosroes, when
> You neither like Ḥaydar[26] brave the world, nor scorn it like Salmān![27]
> Not in the glittering modern world is that contentment to be found:
> It is the splendour of the true believer, his ladder reared on faith.
> When the eagle spirit is awakened in the youth,
> Its destination appears to it far off in the skies.
> Hope on! In despair is the decline of mind and soul,
> The true Believer's hopes are among the confidants of God.
> Your resting-place is not in the vaulted palace of the kings,
> You are a falcon; build your nest upon the mountain rocks.

Iqbal feels deeply hurt when he sees Muslim young men are influenced more by alien ideologies than Islam. In his poem *Falsafa-zada Syed Zade Ke Nam* ("To a Philosophy-stricken Son of Syed") he writes:

> Had you not lost your Selfhood,
> You would not be a slave to Bergson,
> The end of intellect is non-presence,
> Philosophy is removal from life.
> The soundless notes of thought,
> Are death for the love of action.
> By faith the way of life is sustained,
> Faith is the secret of Muḥammad and Ibrāhīm.
> Hold fast to the teachings of Muḥammad,
> You are the son of ʿAlī, from Bu ʿAlī keep away;
> Since the discerning eye you do not posses,
> The Leader of the Quraysh is better than that of Bukhāra.

Iqbal holds the modern educational system responsible for the moral and spiritual decay of the Muslims. He says that the younger generation is devoid of inner warmth and lacking in piety. They

are sharp but unrepentant and do not fear God.
> The eye that is bright with collyrium of the West,
> It's alluring; it's eloquent, but not moist.

He lays the blame on the modern educational institutions. Another source of evil is the excessive rationalism, which kills the spirit by promoting gain and expediency.

Yet another cause of moral and intellectual degeneration is immoderate materialism and an exaggerated reliance on worldly means and resources and the deplorable habit of regarding unemployment and the earning of place and position to be the end of education.
> O high-soaring bird, death is preferable to the sustenance,
> Which clips the wings and arrests the flight.

The main drawback of the modern education is that it is governed by *Maʿāsh* (material life) and not *Maʿād* (Futurity) which takes away the essence of the soul.
> It stole the song from the nightingale's breast,
> And the old fire from the tulip's blood;
> Of this school and learning you are proud,
> Which placed not bread in the hand but took away life.

Mercilessly, but accurately Iqbal exposes the evil characteristics of modern education. Excessive emphasis on means of subsistence, undue expediency, artificial culture and imitative living are its only gifts to mankind.
> The Modern Age is your Angel of Death,
> Deprived you of soul by giving anxiety for bread.
> Your schooling has estranged you from lofty ideas,
> That forbade the mind from toiling at evasion.
> Nature endowed you with a falcon's sight,
> Slavery stuffs a wren's eyes in your sockets.
> The school has hidden from them all secrets,
> That are laid bare in the solitudes of hill and desert.

One of Iqbal's grievances against modern education is that it breeds self-indulgence, passivity and inaction and converts the

ocean of life into a stagnant pool. His prayer for the student is:
> God bring you acquainted with some storm,
> The waters of your sea are tideless and still.

The modern educational system, again, serves as an instrument of Western Imperialism in the East. It promotes the thoughtless imitation of Western customs, practices and ideals and paves the way for colonialism. It forces the Western mental attitudes upon the people of the Orient and creates new problems under the banner of social and economic advancement. By undermining the age-old Eastern values and traditions it seeks to give rise to a society, which, in the words of Macaulay, is Eastern in name and origin but Western in content and reality.

Western atheism and intellectual anarchy instils the same ills and evils into the minds of the young and engenders scepticism, discontent and turmoil in the guise of rationalism and freethinking. In Iqbal's view, blindness is better than a distorted vision and ignorance is preferable to scholarly ungodliness.
> Take it from me that the blind
> Is better than him whose vision is crooked.
> Take it from me, the good-doing simpleton
> Is better than the sage who denies God.

Iqbal repeatedly questions the usefulness of scientific achievements that may enable man to conquer space and fly in the air but sweep him off his feet and dislodge him from his spiritual moorings.
> Of what use the sky-measuring intellect,
> Which revolves around the stars and planets.
> And floats aimlessly in the boundlessness of the atmosphere,
> Like a speck of cloud on the shoulders of the wind?

The contemporary educational system tends to reduce the worth and value of man and emphasise instead machines, industries and other manifestations of material progress although he is the "desired pearl of the ocean of creation" and the "gathered crop of the cornfield of existence." The world should be subservient to man not man to the world.

> Put down not the lamp of desire from your hand,
> In the state of yearning and rapture;
> Lose not your Ego on the world's crossroad.
> Destroy the crossroad and return to yourself.
> Draw both the worlds to yourself,
> Not that you ran away from your existence;
> See your present in the light of the past,
> Today from yesterday none can separate.
> You bear no resemblance to the man of God,
> He, a master of the universe, you a slave;
> Present in you not even the quest of the shore,
> He within him possesses the depths of the oceans.

Without heavenly favour and Divine revelation, human understanding will forever remain imperfect. To make it free and unrestrained before the attainment of maturity is to invite impulsiveness and perversity. Iqbal has written an illuminating *Qita*[28] under the title *Azadi-i-Fikr* ("Freedom of Thought"). It reads:

> Freedom of thought for them is ruinous,
> Who do not possess a disciplined mind.
> If mind is immature, freedom of thought,
> Is the way to make a man a beast.

The manner in which unripe ideologies are becoming widespread in the East and ill-digested ideas are giving rise to mental discontent in the world is also the outcome of the craze of calling everything philosophy.

> People of the seminary entangled in labyrinth of their learning,
> Who, in the Modern Age, cares to keep the count of good and ill?

In another poem entitled *Asr-i-Hazir* ("Modern Age"), Iqbal points out the fundamental drawbacks of both Orient and the Occident. He says that the hate and impatience of the technological Age has destroyed the solidity of everything and reduced philosophy to a haphazard collection of incoherent ideas. Love had failed to find to find its rightful place in the Western way of living because of atheism, whereas intellect had not been able to attain its rightful place in the East because there was no consistency of thought in it.

> Mature ideas, fully developed thought where is one to seek?
> The climate of the present times keeps everything unripe.
> The school gives the reign to the intellect but,
> Love leaves the ideas vague, inconsistent, disordered,
> Love is dead in the West thanks to the atheistic bent of mind,
> Intellect in the East is servile owing to inconsistency of thought.

Modern education encourages a blind infatuation of the West among the youth, killing all spirit of originality or independent action. The world itself is a slave to convention, but the educational institutions are even more narrow and bigoted. They are places where men of exceptional academic ability take pride in being deserters and opportunists instead of functioning as leaders of their Age.

> If the culture of the rubies of Badakshan[29] be the aim,
> The reflection of the wayward sun is futile,
> The world in the web of convention is caught,
> Of what worth the school, the endeavour of the scholars?
> Those who could as leaders of their Age function,
> The dotards, alas, have become its slaves.

Iqbal maintains that the Muslim youth has no existence of its own; it is a shadow of the West and even the artificial life it leads is borrowed. The new generation is a structure of flesh and matter hammered into shape by the artisans of the West but into which they have not breathed the soul. Iqbal bitterly remarks that in the sight of the young the existence of God is a myth but in his view their own existence is shadowy and unreal.

> Your being takes all its light from Europe:
> You are the four walls her architects have built.

> But mud untenanted is the edifice,
> An empty scabbard embellished with flowery gilt.
> To your mind God's existence stands not proved,
> Your own existence is unproved, to mine.
> This only is life-the Self's spark shining out;
> Take heed to it! I do not see your shine!

The Western educational scheme has crushed the spirit of the Muslim youth and instead of firing it with hope and ambition filled its soul with distress and disgust. It has taught the young men to live ostentatiously, made them soft and effeminate and rendered them incapable of standing up to the challenge of life. Iqbal regards the education to be worthless and ill prepares the youth for life.

Iqbal fervently appeals to the teachers and mentors of the rising generations and takes the agony and the grief of the entire *Millet* onto his shoulders in the sentiments expressed in the following verse:

> O old man of *Ḥaram*! Give up the habits of monastery,
> Understand the significance of my morning wail,
> May Allah keep thy young men safe,
> Impart to them the lesson of Selfhood, self-denial,
> Teach them the ways of piercing the rock,
> The West has taught them the art of glass blowing,
> Two hundred years of slavery have broken their hearts,
> Think out some remedy for their confusion now,
> I speak out thy secrets in the paroxysm of madness,
> Make some allowance for my distress too.

CHAPTER FIVE

KNOWLEDGE AND LEARNING

Iqbal's views on knowledge and learning were completely original as they stemmed from his own mental and spiritual awareness. He felt that the aptitude for poetry and literature and the refinement of taste were God-given gifts which could bring about a revolution in the lives of men. People could be roused through them to launch a heroic struggle against the depravity of the environment and to revive and establish sound and healthy values and traditions. The poet or writer's pen, should, therefore, possess the quality of the "rod," the "luminous hand" of Moses and the "breath" of Jesus. He should be willing and able to guide and uplift mankind through love and compassion as well as anger and sternness.

Literature produced merely for emotional satisfaction or induced by an unworthy sentiment is a waste of time and energy and serves no useful purpose. It is misconceived as well as misdirected. In one of his poems, Iqbal says that he is not indifferent to the appreciation of beauty, and recognises that it is a natural instinct. However, if such excessive literature is incapable of evoking a positive and energetic response in the people of a society then it does little good. For what transforms poetry into magic and magic into miracle is the restlessness, warmth and vitality of a living heart. Unless the rich, warm blood of life flows through the lines of a poem it can neither move the hearts nor inspire the minds. With deep anguish he asks poets, writers and artists what is the point of having such a thirst for knowledge if it fails to reach the reality of things. What purpose can the passionate lyrics of the poet or the magical compositions of the musician serve if they do not awaken the hearts and impart life to the atmosphere?

> Valuable is the taste for Art, ye men of vision,
> But vision that perceives not the reality is worthless.
> The goal of Art is the flame of immortal life,
> Not a spasm or two that vanishes like sparks.
> O "rain of spring" if thy produce no tumult in the ocean's bosom,
> What is the worth of that shell and pearl?
> The song of the poet or the minstrel's strain-
> Worthless is the zephyr that makes the garden depressed.
> Without a miracle nations do not rise in the world,
> What Art is devoid of the striking power of the Rod of Moses?

When Iqbal observes the intellectual poverty and lack of substance of his contemporaries he is forced to conclude that like the whole of the East, the Muslim World too is obsessed with sex. The poets and writers of the World of Islam are constantly engrossed in the thought of woman, the musicians never tire of singing her praises, the sculptors carve her images in clay and stone and the artists see the reflection of her beauty at all places. A new intellectual concept of *Waḥdatul Shuhūd* (the Unity of Manifestation) has replaced the traditional pantheistic doctrine of *Waḥdatul Wujūd* (the Unity of Being) in which the world begins and ends with the woman. Iqbal has condemned the vulgar sensualism of the intellectuals and artist in these words:

> Their fantasy the death-bed of love and passion,
> In their dark brains the nations lie entombed,
> In their studios Death's portrait is made,
> The art of these high priests sickens of life,
> They hide from mortal eyes the life's high places,
> Arouse the flesh; put the spirit to sleep:
> Oh, India's painters, poets, storywriters!

The woman sits astride on their nerves.

With regards to philosophy and other intellectual sciences, Iqbal's viewpoint is illustrative of his general approach to life. He believes that an ideology that is not sustained by the spirit of active effort and the sentiment of sacrifice cannot last. If a system of thought confines itself to abstract reasoning, speculative hair-splitting or metaphysical pattern-weaving and shies away from looking at real life and grappling with social realities it is bound to shrivel up and lose its validity.

> Philosophy not written with the blood of heart,
> Is either dead or in the throes of death.

Iqbal's wide study and experience of the world had taught him that it was useless to look to philosophy for the solution of problems fundamental to human existence. Philosophy had no guidance to offer mankind in its struggle for survival and advancement. For a comprehensive programme of life Iqbal falls back upon the message of Islam. He commends his own example to a rationalist friend. He says:

> I came from the stock of idolaters and my ancestors used to worship the pagan deities. There is Brahmin blood in my veins. Yet I came out of the fold of infidelity and embraced Islam. You, on the other hand, are of Hashimite descent and related by blood to the "Leader of the ancients and the moderns."[30] The high distinction of being the Prophet's progeny belongs to you. But having renounced him you are groping in the labyrinth of unproved ideas and vain conjectures, while I (Indian philosophy may be said to be the marrow of whose bones) hold rationality to be the "veil of truth" and the opiate which causes the weakening of the moral and physical fibre of man and makes him an escapist. Even Hegel is as empty-handed, speculative and as hypothetical as anyone. The flame of the heart burns no more in your life; you have lost your Individuality, hence, have become the camp follower of Bergson. What the world needs is the message of life which philosophy does not posses. The Believer's *adhān* is the call of

awakening that arouses the world from sleep and illumines it. Only the legacy of Muḥammad and Ibrāhīm (may the peace and blessings of God be upon them) can bring about order and organisation in faith and life. O Son of ʿAlī, how long will you follow in the steps of Avicenna! The Leader of the Quraysh is far more worthy of allegiance than the leader of Bukhāra. Hold fast to the teachings of Muḥammad, You are the son of ʿAlī, from Bu ʿAlī keep away.

Modern education has been a failure. It has not succeeded in raising up a generation, which could employ its knowledge to lay the foundation of a healthy society in which man was at peace with himself. It possesses a great knowledge of the world but pays little heed to the discovery of humanity and the awareness of Self. It has learnt to control and use steam, electricity and nuclear power but has no idea of its own strength. It has subjugated the world but taken no steps to discipline itself. The modern man flies in the air and swims in the water but cannot walk properly on the earth.

Contemporary education has disturbed the moral and emotional balance of youth. The modern man is equipped with the power but lacking in vision. Iqbal sorrowfully remarks that, "the conqueror of the solar radiation could not brighten his own destiny, the seeker of the orbits of the stars could not chalk out a course of action for himself and the master of science could not mark the difference between good and evil."

> He who enchained the sunbeams could not,
> Unfurl the dawn on life's dark night.
> He sought the orbits of the stars, yet could not,
> Travel his own thought's world;
> Entangled in the labyrinth of his learning,
> Lost count of good and ill.

An ideal Muslim young-man according to Iqbal is a man of unblemished character, whose youth is clean and spotless. His blow is deadly and he is as strong as a lion in war and as soft as silk in peace. He acquits himself well both in combat and in friendship and whilst gentle in speech, he is stern in action. His desires are few and his aims are high. Such a man is contented in poverty and rich in indigence, self-respecting in want and benevolent in prosperity. He prefers death to a life of dishonour. Sometimes, he is the dew that cools the heart of the tulip, and, sometimes, the storm that causes an upheaval in the bosoms of the oceans. He turns into a raging torrent if the mountains beset his path and passes like a singing brook through the bedchamber of love. He is an embodiment of Abū Bakr's faith, ʿAlī's valour, Abū Dharr's contentment and Salmān's devotion. His faith is a lamp of guidance in the dark night of the wilderness and his life is an example of manly courage and fortitude, of *Mu'min*'s wisdom and foresight. He likes martyrdom better than worldly power and rule. The loftiness of his character is the envy of the angels and his existence is a challenge to falsehood and infidelity. Even the whole world cannot pay his price nor can he be bought by anyone except by his Lord. His noble ideals have lifted him above the triviality of the world and its empty allurements. The deceptions of sound and colour mean nothing to him and he refuses to follow and imitate the peacocks and nightingales of the modern civilisation, disdainfully proclaiming:

> Nightingale is nothing but sound,
> And peacock no more than colour.

CHAPTER SIX

ART AND ARCHITECTURE

For Iqbal, Fine arts are just as important as the more serious and productive branches of human skill and endeavour. He regards the artists to be the teachers of humanity who possess the ability to bring about apostolic revolution. Iqbal is opposed to the use of aesthetic abilities for petty gain and cheap entertainment and instead would like to see them brought into play for the growth and development of the Ego.

Instead of getting involved with the external phenomena and immediate object of perception, painting, music and sculpture should try to capture mans' inner richness. Art and learning, faith and wisdom ought to arouse and evolve the latent potentialities of the human personality. Iqbal rejects the idea of a closed and predetermined universe and the sign of a decadent belief of literature, according to him, is that it gets divorced from reality and shuts its eyes to the hard facts of life.

> Music and poetry, statecraft and knowledge, faith and art,
> All of them possess a matchless pearl.
> If they protect the Ego they're the essence of life,
> And if they don't, fiction and witchery.
> Nations in the world have come to grief,
> When faith and literature with Selfhood have parted.

Iqbal is not intolerant of fine arts. He does not question their usefulness, but gives them their proper place. He sincerely appreciates the creativity of the artists but with the difference that poetry, literature and philosophy take precedence in his judgement, over music, sculpture and architecture because they have their roots in thought and intellect.

> Radiance of modern Age is from freshness of thought,
> Bricks and stones do not the worlds make.
> The courage of those who delve into Ego,
> Has from this stream-produced oceans without end.
> The vicissitudes of time he alone overcomes,
> Who with every breath creates life eternal.

Just as Iqbal has his own way of using terms like '*Ilm-o-Ishq* (reason and love), '*Aql-o-Dil* (mind and heart), *Faqr-o-Khudi* (contentment and Ego), *Qalandari-o-Shahini* (detachment and falconism) in the same manner his *Junūn* (frenzy) is not without understanding and judgement. He employs it to indicate the ecstasy of love and the earnestness of the heart. It signifies the feeling of fulfilment and exaltation which works wonders and causes supernatural deeds to happen. *Junūn*, in Iqbal's phraseology, means the attainment of the most complete state of co-ordination and harmony between the body and spirit for a particular purpose.

> I tell you what the life of a Muslim is,
> It's the height of adventure, culmination of frenzy.

As in life so, also, in fine arts Iqbal likes to see the predominance of *Junūn* and utmost sincerity and application on the part of the artist. But for the blossoming of love and frenzy it is not necessary to go into wilderness. They can thrive in society as well.

> Who knows *junūn* has other glories too,
> Provided it is not confined to forest and hill.
> In the overcrowded school it can thrive,
> Wilderness, not at all, is essential for it.

In another *Ghazal* he says:

> I have seen such *junūn* also,
> That has stitched the destiny's events:
> Perfect in the art of drunkenness is he,

Whose intoxication depends not on wine.

In one article, Iqbal elaborates on his views on art and literature, remarking that the first duty of an artist is the affirmation of individuality because "immortality" is achieved only through the expression of the Ego and the affirmation of existence. The artist should start from his own being in order to reach the heart of the universe. He must not neglect Selfhood in the states of "unity in diversity," "privacy in company" and "collective selflessness," for the material world is always eager to absorb everything like clay. Works of art and literature can be said to be eternal when the onward movement from the matter to the spirit is evident. Iqbal, also, feels that the artist should seek out the possibilities of beauty within himself and not in the external phenomena.

> To seek beauty beyond oneself is erroneous,
> What we are after lies not in front.

In other words, art should not stop at answering the question of what it is. It should, rather, go ahead and concern itself with what it should be or become.

> Though not Infidelity, it's not much removed from it either—
> That in the present and the apparent, man of Truth be caught;
> Despair not! Many a revolution is still to come,
> The blue revolving dome is not bereft of new stars.

Iqbal regards the zest for living, earnestness of love and awareness of the Self to be the pre-requisites of the affirmation of existence.

> O thou! Under the sky whose effulgence is like a spark,
> Who can tell thee what the stages of Existence are?
> Art which is devoid of the substance of Ego,
> Alas! For sculpture, poetry and music!
> School and seminary nothing but non-existence teach,
> Learn to Exist for though art and shalt be!

The artist should know himself before he can attain the stage of the realisation and bold affirmation of Selfhood. The development of the Ego cannot materialise before, what Iqbal calls the blending of *Naaz* (capriciousness) with *Nayaz* (humbleness) and the turning away of the drop from the ocean. The limit of Iqbal's sensitiveness is that he describes the *Sajda*[31] in *Namaz* to be symbolic of Selflessness and *Qiyām*[32] of Selfhood and wishes to preserve the individuality of submission even in the absorption of prayer.

> Thy half-opened eyes are still faulty of vision,
> Thy Existence, even now, a mystery to thee;
> Thy humbleness is still unadorned with coquetry,
> For thy *Namaz* even now, is devoid of *Qiyām*,
> The strings of thy Ego's harp are still broken,
> For thou art, even now, ignorant of Rūmī's song.

The poet frowns upon the art which leads one away from life and destroys Selfhood. In this kind of art the material world is the ultimate end and purpose and man is treated as a plaything. He dislikes the modern theatre and opera for the reason that they are soulless and artificial. In them man becomes the *Tamasha* (show; spectacle) and the world becomes the *Tamashaee* (spectator).

> The shrine of thy existence is incandescent with Selfhood,
> What is life but Ego's joy, heat and permanency?
> Higher than the moon and Plaedias its place,
> From its light thy being and attributes.
> The receptacle thine, the Ego of another, God forbid!
> Revive not the trade of [the idols] Lāt and Manāt.
> The triumph of drama that thou ceaseth to be,
> If thou art gone, neither ego's warmth remains nor life's music.

Likewise, Iqbal wants painting to convey the message of the development of human personality. The spiritual content of the Oriental art pleases him but he is repelled by the modern abstract art of the West. He relishes the portrayal of nobler thoughts and sentiments and his love of the beauty, warmth and spirituality depicted in eastern art is very clear.

Art and Architecture

> What grieves me is that modern sculptors,
> Have lost the eternal ecstasy of the east.
> You have perceived Nature and unveiled it too,
> Show your Selfhood in its mirror then.

Music should pulsate with life and express of the excitement, fire and flame of the heart. Iqbal likes the blood of the musician to flow into the chords of his instrument. He should not only be a master of pitch and rhythm but also possess a feeling heart and a sensitive soul.

> Wherefore did the quality of wine come in the wail of flute?
> From the heart of the flautist? Or, from reed?
> What heart is? From where is its strength derived?
> How does its throb overturn the throne of Chosroes?
> Why in its life is the life of nations?
> Why from moment to moment its state alters?
> The empires of Syria, Rome and Rai —why are they,
> Not worth a dime in the sight of a man of heart?
> The day the minstrel understands the mysteries of heart,
> Know that all the stages of art are reached.

What Iqbal seeks is the eternal and timeless song which is not temporary like a flash of the "lightning of destruction" but a "miracle of survival and permanence."

> The wonderhouse of moon and stars may vanish,
> You should remain, and your ethereal song.
> The doctors of Selfhood regard which as lawful,
> The melody is still in quest of a minstrel.
> If the message of death be in music concealed,
> Forbidden in my eyes are rebeck, harp and flute.
> With his breath he poisons the tune,
> The musician whose heart is impure.

Iqbal condemns the music and sculpture which sees the spirit of man as the "fine arts of the slaves." He believes that song and music do not instil life but deal out death by sapping the energies and producing the tendency to avoid the undesirable realities by indulging in pleasant fantasies. Because of them the tenderness of the heart degenerates into feelings of melancholy and life-weariness. They do not even bestow the pain, which obliterates all suffering. The healing touch is missing in them because they are immersed in pessimism and despair.

Music should sweep away all the traces of sorrow and depression. It should be nourished by the sweet madness of love and steeped in the blood of the heart. The glory of music is that it transcends sound and modulation and enters into the realm of the infinite.

> D'you know in music there comes a stage,
> When speech flourishes without the aid of words?

Music without a message is meaningless, and message, in the words of Maulana Rūmī, is what makes the listeners become noble and what protects them against enslavement.

> Meaning is what, by itself, seizes you,
> Makes you indifferent to form and contour.
> Meaning is not what makes a man purblind,
> And heightens the effect of pattern and style.

Iqbal feels that modern sculpture is distinguished neither by the spirit of Ibrāhīm nor by the art of Āzar but is simply crazy. What goes on in its name is the carving and chiselling of death. If the sculptor does not possess the affirmation of faith he simply wields his chisel and hammer without a sense of purpose. There is no spirit of seeking in him, nor the will to create. He is simply a wage earner and a slave to popular preference, possessing no feeling or judgement of his own. The sculptor seeks beauty in the external manifestations of nature while it is, essentially, an inner experience.

The artist who views man and the universe from the same angle and regards them both to be only product of water and clay fails to do justice to himself and thus, his works always lack originality, both in conception and design.

> The moment man supposed himself to be of the earth,

Art and Architecture

> The light of Divinity within him died.
> As Moses out of Selfhood stepped,
> His hand was darkened and staff became a rope.
> Life without the miraculous is not anything,
> But this secret to everyone is not known.

The artist should not only unveil nature but also make an improvement on it through the supernatural element within him and lay the foundations of a new existence. He should try to fill the void in life by putting his own soul into it.

> To remove every inadequacy is your glory,
> With the fullness of your soul.
> Criterion of good and evil is your conscience,
> Your art, the mirror of vice and virtue.

Before the artist embarks upon the conquest of the world he should know himself and develop his Ego. When the individual fulfils himself, he rises above the cosmos and becomes a vital part of the grand design of creation.

> Set down the foot not slowly in the woodlands of desire,
> Seize the world that within you lies.
> Weak and vanquished? Overcome yourself and be triumphant,
> If you are in search of God seek yourself out.
> Skilled in case you are in self-conquest,
> Conquest of the world will be easy for you.

Iqbal likes architecture more than anything else. However, as with art, music and literature, he is more impressed by structures which convey a definite message and whose foundations are laid in love. He sees the Palace of Al-Hamra in Spain but it makes little impression on him even though he is enchanted by the Mosque of Cordova. "The Al-Hamra," he says, "did not impress me much but the visit to the Mosque of Cordova made an impact on my feelings the like of which I had not experienced before."

Similarly, the Mosque in Paris did not fascinate him, as it was nothing other than a piece of architectural elegance.

> What should my eyes see of architect's skill?

> This shrine of the West knows nothing of God;
> Is it a mosque? Nay, the spell-weavers of the West,
> Have smuggled an idol-hall's soul in its carcass.
> And who built this palace of idols?
> The same robbers whose hands have turned Damascus into a desert.

The ruins of *Masjid-i-Quwatul Islam*, built by Qutbuddin Aibak, produce a lasting effect on his mind since they tell of the deep sincerity and resoluteness of the days when Islam had first made its mark in India.

> What in my unilluminated breast is left?
> Lā Ilāh[33] is dead, frustration rife, enthusiasm gone.
> Even Nature's eye will recognise me not,
> The place of Mahmud is different from that of Ayaz.[34]
> Why should of thy massiveness the Muslim not be ashamed?
> Years of servitude, have they not turned him into a rock?
> Worthy of thee is the *Namaz* of the true Believer,
> In whose *Takbīr*[35] battle between Existence and Non-Existence is fought.
> Gone from me is the warmth of feeling,
> Without effulgence is my prayer and invocation.
> My *Adhān* is bereft of grandeur and sublimity,
> In the *Sajdah* of such a Muslim acceptable to thee?

Iqbal feels that the buildings constructed by Qutbuddin Aibak, Sher Shah and Shahjahan possess the spirit of 'the architecture of the free-born' and says that it is easy to see that the builders of these magnificent monuments have given expression to their individuality in them. They have compressed an age into a moment. From their massiveness their viewer acquires firmness of character. Contained in their bricks and stones are the virtues of high-mindedness, manly courage and determination, "Whose places of genuflexion are these stones?" Iqbal asks in wonderment and, then, he cries out, "Don't ask me! Men of the heart alone can tell what passes in the soul. I know only this much that a forehead not adorned with the lance of *Illallāh* is not worthy of prostration in this shrine."

> In me not the lance of *Illallāh*,
> Unworthy of this shrine am I.

In the same way, Iqbal pays a glowing tribute to the Taj Mahal. "Looking at the Taj on a moonlit night," he says, "It appears that its marble slabs are flowing like water and a moment spent here is more lasting than eternity. Here love has revealed its secret through the stones and pierced them with the points of eyelashes. Heavenly music is bursting forth from them and love has attained immortality by passing beyond the range of time and space. It is love, which gives, wings to man and endows his emotions with loftiness and effulgence. It sharpens the intellect and transforms the stone into a mirror. By love the hearts of men of feeling become seats of Divine splendour like the Valley of Sinai and the artists acquire the luminous hand [of Moses]."

Another characteristic of Iqbal's conception of art is that he regards *Jamāl* (beauty) not to be different from *Jalāl* (majesty) but only an aspect of it. Beauty without power is unthinkable to him.

> Belovedness without subdual is wizardry,
> Belovedness with subdual, Apostleship.
> The beginning of love and ecstasy is subdual,
> The end of love and ecstasy is belovedness.
> Which shines from the forehead of man of God,
> The essence of creation is pervaded by the same majesty.
> The poem whose message is eternal life,
> Is Gabriel's song, or Serapheal's trumpet-note.
> In the same eye is power and subdual,
> In the same is beauty and loverhood.

Iqbal has explained his viewpoint at length in the poem called *Jalal-o-Jamal* ("Power and Beauty").

> For me the strength of Ḥaydar is enough,
> The sharpness of Plato's intellect is your fortune.
> With me the meaning of beauty and elegance is,
> That before power the key is bowing low.
> Without power beauty is not worth a straw,

Melody without fire is mere breath.
As punishment even the fire is not acceptable to me,
Whose flame is not unruly, wilful, and headstrong.

If the artist is to fulfil his mission he should be sensitive and possess the power of discernment and penetration. This is the hallmark of a true artist. He must be capable of beholding beauty without a veil. His art should be vitalising and uplifting and by looking at the bright side of things he can then provide guidance to mankind. Art is not only the mirror of life but also its test and standard of judgement. The artist not only observes but also evaluates. The true function of artistic effort is not to delight the audience but to create a new world and make an improvement on nature.

The world does not conceal its nature,
Each atom on self-revelation is bent.
The business of love seems entirely different,
If the eye be blessed with the vision of love.
With it the sons of enslaved nations,
Have risen in the world to rule and govern.
With this eye my frenzy is teaching,
To every dust-particle ways of desert trotting.
If you do not possess the vision of love,
Your existence is a disgrace to heart and eye.

Speaking of the individuality of the artist Iqbal remarks:

His outlook is different from his Age,
Of his state saints and sages unaware.

The artist is his own world. Before he reconstructs the external world a new world must come alive within him and he then must give shape to the images and ideas that pass through his mind in such an inspired state.

The quintessence of Destiny is not hidden from a living heart,
It sees the image of the New World in dream;
And when the *Adhān* awakens him from sleep,
He builds the world as he had seen in dream;
The body of the New World the grime of his palm,

And its soul his mighty Takbīr
Deliver Art from the serfdom of Nature,
Hunters the artists are, not prey.
If you can see the world with your own eyes,
The skies are illumined with the light of your dawn.

We have already seen how Iqbal emphasises the need of sincerity, perseverance and dedication in the artist, not only natural aptitude. Art is demands single-minded application and Iqbal does not believe in the approach of being "tutored by God"

Blood of the heart is the merchandise of life,
Life, Oh fool, is *Lahu-tarang* not *Jal-tarang*.[36]
The vicissitudes of time he alone overcomes,
Who with every breath creates life eternal.
The goal of art is the flame of immortal life,
Not a spasm or two that vanish like sparks.
Only by the toil of flight is the truth revealed,
That earth from the heavens is not far apart.
No such world exists underneath the sky,
Where the throne of *Kai*[37] is seized without a struggle.
Each moment a new *Tūr*[38] and a new epiphany,
May the episode of love never come to an end.
Oh Iqbal! These are the days of rock hewing,
Beware of what through the mirror is shown!
Much as creativeness is God-given,
Men of skill are not free from effort.
From the warmth of mason's blood is construction,
Be it the tavern of Hafiz or Behzad's idol-hall.
Without patient effort merit is not revealed,
The home of Farhad is lit up with sparks of his axe.

CHAPTER SEVEN

THE PERFECT MAN

Even though we live in a depraved world that tries to tempt and allure us at every step, Iqbal does not give up looking for the perfect man. He begins his quest in the long Persian poem, the *Asrar-i-Khudi*, with these verses from Maulana Jalāluddīn Rūmī.

> Last night the Sheikh wandered about the town with a lamp,
> Saying, "I am tired of demon and beast; man is my desire.
> My heart is sick of the feeble-spirited fellow travellers,
> The lion of God[39] and Rustam-i-Dastan[40] are my desire."
> I said, "We too searched for him but he couldn't be found."
> He replied, "What cannot be found—that thing is my desire."

On a dark night, Maulana Rūmī narrates, a man of great wisdom was wandering the streets of the town with a lamp in his hand, as if he was searching for something that had been lost. The poet asked him what he was trying to find and he replied that he had grown sick of living in what, in truth, was the abode of wild animals and was now looking round for a young, deep-hearted man who could revive his sagging spirits and restore his faith in humanity. The poet remarked, "You are sadly mistaken. What you are looking for does not exist. You are wasting your time. I too left no stone unturned in seeking him out but to no avail. Not a trace of him could be found." "It is the rare, the uncommon, and the unattainable that I seek," replied the sage.

Now, did Iqbal succeed in his quest? Was he able to find the man of his dreams, the perfect man, who had realised his transcendental Self? From Iqbal's poems it is clear that he was eminently successful. He not only found the "lost" man but also spent long years of his life in his company. Iqbal's discovery was even more important than the discovery of the New World by Columbus. It was a glorious achievement and a manifest victory for the world particularly in the present times when man had ceased to exist and humanity had become a farce.

Iqbal's perfect man is not different from a true and sincere Muslim who makes his life conform to the general pattern of the Quran and attains the highest degree of perfection by living up to it honestly in every way. He is distinguished from fellow men by the undying quality of his faith and it is his unconquerable spirit of belief, which draws the line between him and the rest of mankind. He outshines them in courage and spiritual stamina and his monotheism separates him from the worshippers of men and glory. His humanitarianism and the universality of his outlook are not limited by race and geography. He possesses the programme of an ideal life and abides by it scrupulously. Even if society's values change and its structure altered he remains loyal. In the words of the Quran, he is like *a good tree, its roots set firm, its branches reaching into heaven* (QURAN, 14:24). Iqbal says:

> The point of God's great compass the Believer's firm faith,
> This entire universe else—shadow, illusion, deceit.

The above description of the perfect man brings to our mind the two characteristics of a Muslim, one relating to the physical and the other to spiritual existence. In his physical existence, a Muslim is like any other mortal. He is born, as all men are, grows up as they do and feels hunger and thirst like them. Like them, too, he is sensitive to heat and cold, falls ill and gets well again. In prosperity and poverty, again, he is not different from the rest of mankind. He engages in trade and occupation and loves his family. In brief, in the human state of being a Muslim is governed by the same law of nature as others are. He, as the others, is mortal.

In the spiritual sphere of his existence, a Muslim is endowed with a message, which is the legacy of the prophets. He has his own outlook on life, believes in certain everlasting truths and lives for a definite aim. Looked at from this angle, a Muslim becomes a part of the mystery of existence. He is indispensable to life. The perfect man or ideal Muslim, as such, has the right to live and prosper in the world. It is essential for the preservation of the human society that he lives and thrives. The world needs the true Muslim in the same way it needs air, water and sunshine. If life is dependent on the basic elements of earth, air, fire and water it also cannot do without an ideal faith and a perfect morality based upon the teachings of the prophets. The Muslim is carrying ahead this responsibility as best he can. In the absence of the faithful Believer this message and these ideals will be lost or become an enigma for the world. The man of faith is needed by creation. Generations and communities will rise and pass away, cities will turn into ruins and the ruins will change again into cities, governments will be made and unmade but the ideal Muslim will remain forever.

Iqbal's perfect man, or Superman, is immortal because he is endowed with an everlasting message. An eternal truth is embedded in his heart and his life is spent pursuing this eternal ideal.

> The Muslim shall not perish for by his *Adhān*,
> The secret of Moses and Abraham is revealed.

It does not, of course, mean that every individual belonging to the Muslim community will live permanently. The Muslim Millet is like an ocean in which waves are continually rising and subsiding but its reality remains unchanged.

Iqbal further claims that the Muslim is the object of creation. The world has been created for him and he has been created for God. Whatever the verdict of theological doctors regarding the truth of the celestial tradition that "but for your sake (O Prophet

Muḥammad) We would not have made the heavens and the earth," Iqbal's penetrating eye perceives something that is distinctly unusual. He is clear-sighted enough to go right into the spirit of the Quran and before him appears the Muslim and his noble mission. He also possesses a keen understanding of history and is well acquainted with the values of the world and the properties of things. He feels that the heavens and the earth and all that is contained in them have been created for the true Believer who is God's deputy and the rightful inheritor of the treasures of the world.

> The earth is the stout-hearted Believer's heritage,
> Who is not *Saheb-I-Laulak*, no Believer is he!

In order to bring to fruition the gospel of thought and action the Believer is required to lead a life of constant endeavour. Iqbal is emphatic that a Muslim can not simply exist. He has been put on this earth to change the course of history, to make the world follow his path and to set a new direction for the evolution of human civilisation and invest a new hope into the ailing community. He is responsible for the guidance of mankind and no one is more worthy of the leadership of the world than him. He must not yield to a society which is depraved and ignorant, rather, his job is to raise the banner of revolt and fight against the prevalent evils till he gets his own way. In Iqbal's view the doctrine, "Move in the direction in which the wind is blowing," is not worthy of the Believer.

> The gospel of the faint-hearted: Adapt yourself to the times,
> But you, if the times do not agree, contend with them.

The true Believer does not compromise with the perverted values of life. He has been put here to fight against them and it is his duty to reform and correct mankind and even destruction would be justified, as the aim would be to rebuild the world.

> In whose heart abides the urge to die for Truth,
> He should first instil life into his earthly frame;
> Burn down the borrowed heavens and earth,

And from their ashes create a world of his own.

The Muslim must not seek shelter behind the facades of fatalism and predestination. Only those who are lacking in faith and courage use such excuses. The truthful Believer is the destiny of Allah.

> If a Muslim is without faith, he is a slave to destiny,
> Endowed with faith, he becomes the destiny of Allah.
> Exalt thy Ego so high that before every decree,
> God Himself may ask thee: What is thy wish?

As Iqbal examines the history of the worlds he concludes that the faithful Believer always brings about a healthy and wholesome revolution. He is the leader of revolution and the messenger of life, the *Muezzin* of daybreak after a long night. His *Adhān* breaks the stillness of the worlds, which is as oppressive as the silence of the graveyard and reanimates it. It is the same call that rose from the heights of *Faran*[41] thirteen hundreds years ago and proved to be the note of Raphael's trumpet for the ailing humanity. Even today it is capable of rousing the world and stirring the conscience of man. What is needed is only the Believer who can infuse the spirit of Bilāl[42] into it.

> Which can change the dark night into a sunny forenoon,
> The Believer's *Adhān* is the voice of the firmament.

The *Adhān* of the Believer alone can usher in the morning, which will give rise to a New World

> The morning which is sometimes today and sometimes tomorrow,
> God alone knows from where it comes.
> The morning by which the bedchamber of existence shakes,
> From the *Adhān* the Believer is born.

Iqbal also believes that the strength of the true Believer is supernatural. It cannot be explained by the known laws of nature and must, therefore, be a miracle. He draws a fresh vigour and vitality from his faith, and God's Will, Intention and Might are on his side. Neither mountains nor oceans can block his path.

> The hand of the *Mu'min* is the Hand of Allah—
> Dominant, resourceful, creative, ensuring success;
> Fashioned out of dust and light, slave with the Master attributes,
> His heart is indifferent to the riches of the worlds.

Islamic heroes like Ṭāriq bin Ziyād, the Conqueror of Spain, are the living images of Iqbal's ideal Muslim.

> The *Ghazis*,[43] these mysterious bondsmen of Thine,
> To whom Thou hast granted zest for Divinity.
> Deserts and oceans fold up at their kick,
> And mountains shrink into mustard-seeds.
> Indifferent to the riches of the worlds it makes,
> What a curious thing is the ecstasy of love?
> Martyrdom is the desired end of the *Mu'min*,
> Not spoils of war, kingdom and rule.
> Thou made the desert-dwellers absolutely unique,
> In thought, in perception, in the morning *Adhān*.
> What, for centuries, life had been seeking,
> It found the warmth in the hearts of these men.

Iqbal looks deep into the hidden sources of the *Mu'min's* strength. He exclaims:

> Who can imagine the strength of his arm?
> Destinies change at the glance of the *Mu'min*.

Iqbal's observation is backed up by past events. Many times in the past small bands of truthful Muslims have made history, sweeping away the obstacles that lay before them. The deeds of Muslim heroes like Saʿd ibn Abī Waqqās, Mussana Ibn al-Ḥāritha, ʿAqaba Ibn ʿĀmir, Muḥammad Ibn Qāsim, Mūsā Ibn al-Naṣīr and Ṭāriq Ibn Ziyād are still preserved in the annals of our race.

The *Mu'min* is a world reality, above and beyond the limitations of time and space. He cannot be imprisoned by the boundaries of race, politics or geography.

> Limitless is his world, boundless his long horizon,
> Tigris and Danube and Nile but a wave in his sea;
> His times are wondrous; his legends are strange,

> To the ages outworn he gave the command to depart;
> Saqi of men of taste, horseman of the realm of desire,
> Pure and unmixed his wine, tempered and glittering his steel.

Iqbal's superman is timeless. He belongs to no particular place or country for the whole world is his home.

> God intoxicated Faqir belongs not to East or to West,
> Delhi nor Isfahan nor Samarqand his home.
> Boundless is the world of *Mu'min*
> In all places his home.

Since the world belongs to God, and the Muslim is God's own bondsman, the entire universe is his home.

When Ṭāriq landed at the coast of Spain he ordered the boats in which he and his men had crossed the sea to be burnt so that there remained no possibility of a retreat. Some of his companions expressed their disapproval, "What are you doing?" they protested. "We are far away from home and have to return, after all." The dauntless General, thereupon, smiled, drew his sword and remarked, "What is the question of returning? Every country is our country for it is the country of our Lord and to Him we belong." Iqbal has depicted this memorable event in these words:

> As Ṭāriq burnt the boats at Andalusia's coast,
> His companions protested: "Your act is unwise,
> We are away from home; how shall we return?
> Repudiation of material means the *Sharīʿah* does not permit."
> Ṭāriq smiled, drew his sword, declared:
> "Every country is our country for it's the country of our Lord."

Iqbal's concept of an ideal Muslim shows him as possessing diverse and often contradictory attributes, thus bringing to light his multi-faceted personality. Such different and mutually incompatible qualities are the manifestations of the Divine attributes that are revealed through the true Muslim. When it comes to generosity, mildness and patience, the *Mu'min* is the embodiment of the Divine Attribute of Forgiveness. In respect of sternness of faith, and in severity and anger with regard to falsehood and infidelity he signifies the Divine attribute of subdual whilst in piety and virtuousness he stands for the Divine Attribute of Purity. A Muslim cannot be a true representative of his faith unless he acquires all these qualities.

> Subdual and Forgiveness, Purity and power,
> When these combine a Muslim is born.

The *Mu'min* of this mental and moral greatness is like the shining sun, which never sets. If it goes down in one direction it rises in another.

> Men of faith live in the world like the sun,
> Setting here, rising there, setting there.
> When a calamity has struck some part of the Islamic World,
> Due, no doubt, to our own folly, suitable amends have invariably been made for it elsewhere.

If Islam has suffered a setback at one place, it has gained a notable victory at another. A new star has never failed to appear within Islam whenever darkness has threatened to spread over it. The loss of Spain was an appalling tragedy for the Muslim *Millet*, but at that very time the Ottoman Empire emerged in the heart of Europe. The sack of Baghdad by the Tartars was a gruesome event, but the Muslim Empire in India peaked simultaneously with it. At the beginning of the 20TH Century the Islamic world suffered numerous setbacks at the hands of Europe and it seemed that Turkey was going to be divided by the Allied Powers among themselves as if it had been their ancestral property. However, in the midst of the encircling gloom the Muslims exhibited a remarkable capacity for resurgence. They suddenly became politically active and various movements were initiated in their lands for revival and reform. Today the Muslim World seems to be poised for rebirth and regeneration. The annals of Islam are full of events illustrating the truth of the statement that if its sun has sunk below the horizon on one side its rays have shot forth from the other. It is this way because Islam is the last message of God which is the guidance for all mankind and no other message is going to be sent down after it. The Muslims are the last community to serve as the custodians and preachers of the Divine Word and if they are destroyed the ultimate guidance from on High, too, will perish and humanity will be left to grope and fumble in utter darkness until the Last Day.

The existence of Islam has always posed a threat to impiety and ungodliness. It is the only programme of life that condemns all the fake and hollow ways of living. Godless conduct and the ascendancy of the Devil can continue only until Islam comes into its own and a body of true Believers sets about fulfilling its mission. Iqbal has developed this theme in his excellent poem entitled, *Iblis ki Majlis-i-Shura* ("The Advisory Council of Satan") in which Islam is depicted as the chief source of danger to the infernal order of things. The Devil feels that the more Islamic law and programme of life are hidden from the world's view the better it is for him and all that he upholds. He is thankful that the Muslim is neglectful of his faith and advises his disciples to keep him engrossed in scholastic disputations so that all his "moves on the chessboard of life" are frustrated and he remains a stranger to the "world of action."

> Every moment do I at the thought of their wakening tremble,
> The real purposes of whose faith is the superintendence of the world.

Without doubt, the devoted henchmen of Satan have amply succeeded in their evil designs against Islam. Their chief concern has been to extinguish the faith inside Muslims, to overwhelm them and to deprive them of Islamic courage and vitality in the Arab as well as the non-Arab lands. This is because Islam gives the Muslims courage to carry out superhuman feats of fearlessness and sacrifice in the path of God and keeps them firm and steadfast in the face of heaviest odds. In *Iblis Ka Paigham Apne Siyasi Farzandon ke Nam* ("Satan's Command to His Political

Offspring") Iqbal says:

> The man who raked with hunger fears not death—
> Muḥammad's spirit from his brain expel:
> Put Frankish thoughts into Arabia's mind—
> Islam from Yemen and Hejaz expel:
> Cure for the Afghan's pride of faith?
> The *Mulla*[44] from his mountains and glen expel.

The surest way to do it is to set up an educational system that puts an end to respect for Islam and attachment to its way of life in the hearts and minds of the growing generations of the Muslims. This would, instead engender a materialistic outlook which demoralises them and lays them open to doubts and misgivings and turns them into shameless seekers of physical pleasures. Akbar Allahabadi has sarcastically criticised the educational scheme in the following verse:

> Pharaoh would not have earned notoriety for infanticide,
> Had the idea of founding a college crossed his mind.

Iqbal feels that the forces of darkness and paganism are attaining their desired objective. They are weakening the spirit everywhere, extinguishing the flame of faith and allowing the spirit of *Jihād*[45] to be taken over by greed and materialism.

> In the ardour of Arab's remembrance, in the music of Iranian's thought,
> Observations are neither of Arabia, nor ideas those of Iran.
> Not one Ḥusayn in the caravan of Herjaz is found,
> Tresses of Tigris and Euphrates though are lustrous still.

The pathetic state of Muslims moves Iqbal to tears and he complains:

> O inheritor of *Lā Ilāh!* In you is left,
> The speech of loverhood, nor sternness of character;
> Hearts in breasts trembled at your glance,
> But in you the fire of Qalandar burns no more.

Another place he again expresses his sorrow:

> Prostration at which the earth's soul trembled,

> Pulpit and arch for it are yearning;
> In Egypt and in Palestine I did not hear,
> The *Adhān* that gave the mountain the creeps.
> Pearl of life in thy ocean does not exist,
> I looked for it in every wave and shell.

The Muslims are facing such misery because the spark of faith has gone out of their hearts and they have grown dead to spiritual feeling.

> The madness of love is no more,
> The blood runs in Muslims veins no more;
> Their prayer-ranks broken, hearts distracted, worship spiritless,
> Because their inner passion is no more.

All the same, Iqbal is not disheartened; he is not a pessimistic poet, rather one of faith and hope. He is confident that political shocks, trials and ordeals will rouse the Muslims from lethargy and produce a new impulse of life in them. In *Tulu-i-Islam* (*Dawn of Islam*), for example, he says:

> The faint light of stars tells the daybreak is near,
> The sun has risen, gone the period of heavy slumber.
> In the East's chill veins life-blood flows again,
> Avicenna and Farābī this mystery cannot solve.
> The tempest of West has made the Muslim a true Muslim,
> In the tumult of sea pearl's fulfilment lies.
> To *Mu'min*, again, from the Almighty is going to be granted,
> The dignity of Turk, the intellect of Indian, the eloquence of Arab.

And again,

> Of his desolate sowing-field Iqbal shall not despair,
> A little rain and the soil is most fertile, Oh Saqi!

The Western civilisation had had its day. Signs of decay and disintegration are already noticeable in it. A new civilisation is about to take its place. However, Iqbal is equally convinced that unless truthful Muslims assume the leadership of the emerging world mankind will continue to be treated heartlessly by the crafty gamblers of the West.

THE GLORY OF IQBAL

But now a New World is born, the Old World is dying—
The world dice-throwers of Europe have made a gambling den.

CHAPTER EIGHT

THE PLACE OF THE TRUE BELIEVER

During the days of Maulana Jalāluddīn Rūmī, frustration and despair was rife among the people due to continuous misrule, uninterrupted oppression and endless strife. Man stood disgraced in his own eyes. Iranian mysticism had constantly preached the cult of renunciation; and the awareness of the Self, which is the source of human eagerness and enthusiasm, had come to be looked down upon as immoral and backward-looking. The attainment of the celestial standards of purity and perfection and denial and rejection of the basic human tendencies were praised as the only objectives worth living for. Moreover, celibacy was advocated as a mark of spiritual excellence. Man saw the fulfilment of his destiny not in humanity but in the rejection of it. A general denial of the concept of human dignity and of the ideals and aspirations characteristic to mankind had taken place and this philosophy had also permeated poetry and literature. Owing to obnoxious moral and mental attitudes and lack of appreciation of his own potentiality, man, sometimes, felt inclined to be envious even of the quadrupeds.

Maulana Rūmī saw at once what lay at the root of this and attacked it unsparingly. He preached human superiority and worthiness with such vigour and fervour that the dormant capabilities of man were awoken and he became conscious of the crucial place that he occupied in the universe. The whole of Islamic thought and literature was influenced by the Maulana's teachings and a new trend was set in poetry and mysticism.

After that followed the era of political and cultural ascendancy from the West, which had assimilated ideas of monasticism from the Roman Church and also received its share of the doctrines of the Original Sin and Atonement. Apart from it, in the Western society, thanks to the materialistic system of thought, man was regarded to be a tool of production and an evolved animal whose main purpose in life was to manufacture goods of trade and satisfy his physical appetites.

What followed was that the intrinsic goodness and nobility of man and all the things connected with his inner existence were neglected and he was condemned to the position of a helpless creature before a blind and heartless Providence.

The Muslim East was plunged into despair and confusion. Taken aback by the material achievements of the West, the Muslim surrendered before it and sought refuge in the philosophy of ascetic inaction. They were then not only pushed behind and left to gaze with sentimental melancholy at the tremendous turn of events but also lost faith in themselves and having renounced a life of active effort, began to derive a morbid satisfaction from their misfortune.

The Muslim became the proverbial "sick-man" of the Orient and an exaggerated awareness of his troubles made him worthless in his own eyes. It was in these circumstances that a new political and economic system and unfamiliar intellectual and literary patterns appeared in Asia and Africa. As in the Muslim east, they were shown to deny faith and individuality. These distinctive features of the Western civilisation made man refuse to accept transcendental truths and a deliberate attempt was made to overlook the innate powers and hidden capabilities of the true Believer by means of which he overcame the forces of nature and performed extraordinary deeds. No one had the vision and perspicacity to recognise the worth of the *Mu'min's* fearlessness, magnanimity and sincerity and his contemptuous disregard of artificial values and bold refusal to give in to imaginary fears and ungrounded misgivings.

The Eastern countries had borrowed the decadent concepts of the West without subjecting them to critical examination and had thus become the enthusiastic followers of their masters.

Under these conditions of inert, lazy and weary conditions, Iqbal sings praises of the faithful Believer and advises him to be self-reliant and self-respecting. He shows him that his legitimate place in the scheme of creation is brought about through action and enterprise, leadership and guidance, as well as power, dignity, self-awareness and self-realisation.

In one of his long Persian poems, he addresses the *Mu'min* in these words:

> I am amazed at your state. The skies are irradiant because of you, but you have ceased to be. How long will you lead a life of ignorance and degradation? It was from you that the world received its mental and spiritual illumination. You served as a minaret of light during the dark night of the past. The "luminous hand" [of Moses] was present in your sleeve. But today, you have shut yourself up in a narrow shell and seem to have forgotten that you can break it. You were present before the world was created and will remain after it has ended. You are afraid of death while death itself should be afraid of you. Death is not lying in wait for you but it is the other way round. Man does not die with the departing of the soul. He dies when faith goes out of him and belief deserts his heart.

> The world you see, but Selfhood you can't,
> How long in your ignorance will you sit?
> With your ancient flame illumine the night,
> The hand of Moses is sleeved in you.
> Set forth your foot from the circling skies,
> Greater and older than these you are,
> Your fear death, O imperishable man!
> Death is but a prey that before you lies.
> Life once given none can take,

It is for lack of faith, men swoon and die,
Learn to be a sculptor, even as I,
And haply anew your Selfhood make.

In another poem Iqbal calls upon the Muslim youth to shake off their lethargy and join the battle of life in the spirit of a crusader. He says:

O sleeping bud! Open your eyes like the wakeful narcissus, which never takes a nap nor falls asleep. The enemy has encroached upon our home and rendered us destitute. Will the sound of the nightingale, the call of *Adhān* and the cry of the broken heart not rouse you from slumber? The sun has set out on its journey again, and, in the ocean of darkness the oars of brilliant dayspring have come back into motion. The caravans have packed their luggage in the desert and drums of departure have sounded. But O wakeful eye that was the guardian of mankind and protector of the weak! Thou art still lost in sleep and oblivious of the vast changes that are taking place in the world. Your sea has become motionless. There is no trace of movement in it, no sign of agitation in its waves. What kind of a sea is it that does not contain even one high-rising tide or a monster. Your sea should have swept over its coast and into the hills and plains. O truthful Muslim! Country is like the earthen body while the soul is related to faith. You must, therefore, rise with the word of God in one hand and the unsheathed swords in the other for in their combination lies the good fortune of mankind and the advantage of civilisation. O Believer! You are the custodian of the eternal order and the confidant of Allah. Your arm is the arm of God. Though a creature of clay, the existence of the world is dependent on you. Drink the wine of belief and rise above doubt and uncertainty. Against the deceitful charm of the West there is no redress. I cry mercy against the conjuror, who sometimes allures and sometimes binds in chains; who plays the roles of both Shirin[46] and Parvez.[47] The world has been laid desolate by its despoliation. O founder of Ḥaram! O builder of Ka'ba! O son of Ibrāhīm! Awake out of your deep slumber for the reconstruction of the world.

Little flower fast asleep, rise narcissus-like and see,

The Place of the True Believer

Our bower has been laid waste by cold grief; arise!
By the wail of the nightingale, by the Muezzin's call; arise!
Listen to the burning sighs of the passionate hearts and rise.

Now that the sun has tied its ornament on the brow of morn,
And in its ear put the crimson pendant of its heart's blood,
In the mountain and in the plain caravans have broken camp,
Bright and world-beholding eyes for the surveying world, arise!

All the Orient lies strewn like the roadway's dust,
Like a hushed wail, like a wasted sigh;
Yet each atom of this earth is quickened by a glance,
From Ind and Samarkand, from Iraq and Hamadan rise!

As placid your ocean as only a desert can be,
What an ocean which neither does rise nor ever recedes?
What an ocean that never knows a storm or an alligator possesses?
Rend its breast and like a swelling tide, arise!

Listen to this truth that all mystery reveals,
Empire is the body and true Religion the soul,
Body lives and soul lives by the life their union gives,
With lance and sword, cloak and prayer mat arise!
Out of heavy sleep, heavy sleep arise!
Out of slumber deep arise!

In another Urdu *Ghazal* Iqbal says:

This morning breeze has conveyed the message to me:
Kingship is the lot of those who realise themselves.
Your life is from it and so your honour,
If the Ego endures there is glory, or else disgrace:
In the circle of my poetry are being raised,
Beggars who possess the demeanour of kings;
You are the hunter of the Phoenix; only the beginning it is,
The world of fish and fowl has not been created in vain;
An Arab or a Persian, your There is no God but He!
A meaningless phrase if the heart does not affirm.

The poet, again, exhorts Muslims in these words in a poem of rare simplicity and appeal: "O Believer! All the things that are contained in the heavens and the earth, the planets, the rivers, the mountains and the forests are transitory. Only you are everlasting. Whatever exists in the world has been subjugated to you. But you are sadly ignorant. How long will you run after the world? Either spurn it or make it bend to your will. There is no other way."

> All life is voyaging, all things in motion,
> Moon, stars and fish and fowl!
> Angels and ministering spirits, your soldiers,
> You are the champion, the leader of the army;
> Of your own worth you have no notion,
> Oh that blindness, that insolvency.
> How long the slavery of the world of matter?
> The choice is yours; be a monk or king.

Iqbal never tires of warning Muslim youth against the perils of imitating a civilisation that treats the word not as a thing of the heart and soul and a place for the development of the human Ego, but as a marketplace, a wine shop and gambling den. It is only a field of battle for profit and a theatre of war for overlordship and supremacy.

CHAPTER NINE

SATAN'S ADVISORY COUNCIL

In the final collection of Iqbal's poems called, *Armughan-i-Hejaz* (*The Gift from Arabia*), and published after his death, is *Majlis-i-Shura* (*Satan's Advisory Council*). In it, the poet has used the Devil himself to give artistic expression to his highly characteristic philosophical ideas. The evil spirits of the world are shown to have gathered together in order to ponder over the new developments that are proving a stumbling block to their wicked designs and ambitions. The disciples of Satan put forward their views and suggestions which he examines and, then, gives his own verdict based on a vast experience of men and matters. The henchmen of Satan are deeply impressed by what their leader tells them and they readily accept his assessment of the situation.

Satan's viewpoint is that the Muslim is the real enemy. He is the spark that can, at any time, burst into a blazing flame and destroy the entire demonical system. Therefore, all their resources and energies should be directed against this chief opponent, and if he cannot be annihilated he should, at least, be lulled into a state of complacency and self-dissatisfaction. The portrait of the Muslim is drawn in the poem with consummate skill and profound sensitiveness and the other faiths and philosophies and their leaders have also been discussed. The poem opens with an address by Satan during the course of which he remarks:

> The old game of elements, this lowly world,
> Graveyard of hopes of the dwellers of ninth heaven.

> Towards its destruction the Lord, today, is inclined,
> Who had called it the world of *Be! and it is.*
> I showed the Frank the path of Imperialism,
> The spell of church, mosque and temple I broke.
> To the pauper I taught the cult of fate,
> And to the wealthy the craze of Capitalism I gave.
> Who can cool down the blazing flame?
> In whose fury is the inner heat of Satan?
> Whose branches be high with our watering,
> That ancient tree who can uproot?

After the inaugural address the first adviser says that no one can doubt the stability of the Satanic Order which has firmly established its hold on the king and the beggar alike. The masses are reconciled to their lot and they willingly accept the squalor and wretchedness of their position. Their hearts have grown so insensitive that desire is never born in them, and, if it ever is, it quickly dies or changes into a dream. The adviser asserts that it is due to their sustained efforts that the *Mulla* (theologian) and the *Sufi* (mystic), who enjoys leadership amongst the Muslims, have come to terms with monarchy in which supreme power is vested in an individual. The *Sufi* imagines that spirituality, God-realisation and mysticism—do not extend beyond *Qawwālī* (devotional music) and *Ḥāl* (mystic raptures). In the same way, the learning and scholarship of the *Mulla* is confined to debate and metaphysical subtleties. Those who were entrusted with the religious and spiritual leadership of the people have themselves; become the slaves of tyrannical rulers and sovereigns. The religious ceremonies of Islam are still observed, the Haj pilgrimage and circumambulation of the House of Kaʿba are carried out even now, but the spirit of world leadership and guidance has deserted the Muslims. Their sword has lost its sharpness and the limit of despair is that consensus has been reached among them, so to speak, on the prohibition of *Jihād*.

The Satanic Order is, surely, supreme

Thanks to it, masses in serfdom have matured.
Since eternity prostration has been the lot of the poor,
Their inclination is towards *Namaz* bereft of *Qiyām*.
Ambition, in the first place, is never born,
And if it ever is, it dies or becomes a wishful dream.
The miracle of our endeavour is that today,
Mulla and Sufi are Sovereign's sycophants.
For the Easterner's disposition this opium is best,
Or else, no better than Qawwālī scholasticism is.
What if the Hajj and *Ṭawāf*[48] are still performed,
The unsheathed sword of the Muslim has lost its edge.
Whose defeat is this reasoning, this latest fiat,
Jihād to Muslim is forbidden in the present Age?

The second adviser, then, mentions democracy as the chief cause of peril.

> Clamour for the rule of the people—is it good or evil?
> Of the mischief of present times you are hopelessly unaware.

With regards to this, the first adviser remarks that he sees no danger in democracy, which is only an attractive veil worn by autocracy to hide its ugly face. It is, after all, their own creation, for they have designed the apparel of democracy for monarchical or oligarchic rule:

> When people get tired of despotism and begin to think in terms of freedom and human dignity and we feel that a threat is developing to our supremacy. We try to placate them by placing the doll of democracy in their hands. Popular representatives and elected ministers are only the symbols of autocracy with a different name. Monarchy does not rest with a particular individual. It means the exploitation of man by man and the usurpation of other people's wealth by force or fraud. It has nothing to do with an individual, group or party. The democratic system of the West is not frees from taint. Its outward aspect is bright but inwardly it is as dark as any unjust system of political organisation can be.

> Be it as may, my experience of the world tells,
> Why fear a system, which is monarchy's veil?

> We have dressed up monarchy in democratic attire,
> When man has shown awareness of his rights.
> The reality of monarchic order is different,
> It's not dependent on the existence of kings.
> Be it the House of people or the Court of Parvez,
> Who covets the harvest of others is a king.
> Have you not seen that democracy of the West,
> Is bright outwardly, but inwardly dark as Chengiz?

After this comforting explanation, the third adviser heaves a sigh of relief and says that if it is the case that there is no harm in democracy what answer does one have to the menace of Karl Marx, who without being an Apostle is held in an equal religious reverence by his followers? Marx was undoubtedly a revolutionary by temperament, but since he was not blessed with Divine guidance he ended up as a "Moses without an epiphany" and a "Christ without a crucifix" and failed to give correct leadership and guidance to the world. He rebelled against religion and rejected the scriptures, yet his own book *Das Kapital* is regarded by the Communists as gospel, and is even being regarded as a revealed faith. His doctrine has shaken the world and through the theory of class struggle he has set the proletariat against the bourgeoisie and sown the seeds of hatred among nations.

> Till the spirit of kingship lasts there's nothing to fear,
> But what answer have we to the mischief of the Jew?
> That Moses without a Glimpse, that Christ without a Crucifix,
> No Apostle is he, yet carries a Book under arm.
> How terrible, indeed, is that infidel's piercing glance,
> Day of Reckoning for nations of East and West!
> What perversity is greater than this, I ask,
> Slaves have torn the ropes of their masters' tents?

It is now the turn of the fifth adviser to speak:

Though the conjurors of the West are your own disciples I have not much faith in their wisdom. The Samri Jew[49] [Karl Marx, who is the reincarnation of Mazdak] is playing havoc with the human race. He has bewitched the world so completely that everyone who is inferior in age, rank or position is at loggerheads with those who are superior. Even scoundrels are claiming equality with kings. We, at first ignored the menace but it has been growing day by day and now it has assumed such proportions that the earth trembles at the thought of what lies in store for it. Your leadership in peril and the world on which your authority rests is doomed.

> Conjurors of the West though all your disciples be,
> I have little faith left in their wisdom now.
> The Jewish mischief-monger, the re-incarnation of Mazdak,
> His madness is about to tear every robe into shreds.
> The crow with the falcon equality claims,
> How quickly the temper of time is changed!
> Over the skies frenziedly it has spread,
> What we had thought to be a handful of dust.
> Such awe has this building menace struck,
> That the brooks, the hills and the yonder mountains shake.
> The world, my Lord! Is about to crumble,
> The world that depends upon your leadership alone.

Finally, Satan speaks his mind and lays down a plan of action for the future. "These movements and ideologies," he declares, "hold no terror for me. I am still in control of the affairs of the world. No upheaval takes place anywhere in which I do not have a hand. The world will have a taste of my power the moment I decide to start a war among nations, or, more specially, to warm up the blood of European peoples. Men will then rush at each other's throats like wolves and tear one another to pieces. The spirituality of the ecclesiastics and perspicacity of the statesman will be of no benefit to them once I whisper into their ears. They will begin to behave like lunatics."

Communism does not impress Satan because it strives against nature and seeks to abolish inequality by means of dialectics. How can these idiotic eccentrics frighten him?

> The world of hue and scent I hold in my hand,

> The earth, the planets and the skies, layer after layer.
> The spectacle east and West will, surely, see
> Once I warmed up the blood of nations.
> Leaders of politics, dignitaries of the Church,
> A vocative particle of mine can drive them crazy,
> The fool who imagines the world a glassblower's workshop,
> Let him try to break the goblets of this civilisation!
> Garments that have been by the hands of Providence rent
> By the needle of Mazdakite, dialectics can never be stitched.
> Can the Communist scoundrels strike terror in me?
> The wretched souls distracted in mind, incoherent of speech

Satan adds that if he is afraid of anyone it is the Muslim *Millet* since in them the spark of faith is still hidden. Though, on the whole, it has fallen on evil days there is no lack of outstanding individuals in it. Its solidarity has been destroyed and it is falling to pieces, yet it can still boast deep-hearted men who can alter the course of history and turn defeat into victory. Such men of endeavour and determination are even now found among Muslims who leave their beds before daybreak and devote themselves to Prayer and supplication, whose nights are spent in lamentation, wail and invocation and who perform the *Wuḍū'*[50] with the tears of the early morn. Their midnight worship is their chief weapon. Islam, not Communism, is the menace of tomorrow, the threat of the future.

> If any fear attends me, it is from the people whose ashes yet the spark of Desire contain,
> Occasionally still, I see among the men who work with tears perform the Wuḍū' in the early morn.
> He who knows the secrets of history knows,
> That Communism is not tomorrow's menace, but Islam.

Satan knows that Muslims have deviated from the path of the Quran and have forgotten the Islamic programme of life. The love of worldly possessions and self-seeking has become their creed. He is also aware that the future of the East is very dark for the Ulema of Islam and its leaders do not possess the light that dispels gloom. They do not have the "luminous hand" yet it is quite possible that the demands of time may jolt this community out of its stupor and make it return to Islam. Satan says to his advisers:

> You are ignorant of the efficacy and comprehensiveness of the "faith of Muḥammad" and the *Sharīʿah* of Islam. This glowing, incandescent *Sharīʿah* protects the institution of family, safeguards the rights of men and women, and establishes a clean and healthy society. The creed of Islam is the creed of honour and dignity, purity and trustworthiness, courage and compassion, generosity and large-heartedness and piety and cleanliness. It puts an end to every kind of injustice, falsehood and servility. There are no distinctions of high and low, rich or poor in it. Kings and beggars are alike in its sight. Its system of *Zakāt*[51] is based on a fair and balanced concept of wealth. It treats the worldly goods to be a trust of God and sets down the rights of the poor in them. By the emphatic declaration that the earth belongs to God and not to rulers it has brought about a revolution in the minds of men. Our endeavour should, therefore, be to keep this faith hidden from the view of the world. It is good that the Muslims, themselves, have turned away from the Straight Path and got steeped in mysticism and polemics. Keep the Muslim *Millet* engrossed in sleep by patting it gently lest it woke up and threw the entire Satanic Order into jeopardy with its mighty *Takbīrs*. Let us hold the *Muʾmin* back from the field of action so that he may be beaten on all fronts of life and fail to play his role on the stage of history. The enslavement of the Islamic World is essential for the success of the systems of colonialism and exploitation and the way to do it is to go on administering to the Muslims the dope of poetry, mysticism, contentment and renunciation. The more the Muslim is enamoured by the monastic way of life and remains fond of omens, charms, rituals and ceremonies the more he will be driven away from the world of active effort. Remember that I fear the awakening of the Muslim *Millet* because it means the awakening of the whole of mankind and not a mere community. In this *Millet* the bond between man and the universe is firmly established and self-introspection goes side by side with the close study and supervision of the world.

That from the Quran they have departed, I know,
And Capitalism is now the creed of the Believer.
In the pitch-dark night that upon the East has fallen,
The wise men of *Haram* are without the light of faith.
But from the exigencies of the age I fear,
That the Law of the Prophet! A hundred times beware!
The safeguard of women's honour, tester of men, maker of men.
The voice of death for all forms of slavery,
There is no distinction of the ruler and the ruled in its domain.
It purges wealth of foulness,
And the rich trustees of their goods it makes.
Can a more dreadful thing than this ever be—
The earth belongs to God and not to kings?
The more this Law from the world's view is hidden the better,
Luckily the Muslim himself is devoid of faith.
Let him in meticulous interpretations of the book his energies waste,
And a helpless groper in the gloom of Theology be.
Whose mighty Takbīrs the spell of time and space can break,
May his night of decay no daybreak see!
You keep him a stranger to the world of deed, I say,
That all his moves on life's chessboard be thwarted.
For him such, poetry and mysticism are, indeed, the best,
Which from his eye life's broad spectacle conceal.
Every moment do I at the thought of their awakening tremble,
The real purpose of whose faith is supervision of the universe.

Should fiendish movements and wicked ideologies succeed and a plan of action is drawn up from the annihilation of the Muslims the foremost objective will be to put out the spark of faith that has already become very weak. The Devil and his henchmen will, in the first place, aim at destroying the sense of Islamic dignity and self-respect which arouses the sentiments of *Jihād* in the Muslim *Millet* and induces it to revolt against the forces of evil and injustice. In the poem *Iblis ka Paigham Apne Siyasi Farzandon Ke Nam* ("Satan's Command to His Political Offspring"), Iqbal has drawn attention to it. In it, Satan tells his political children that, "the *Mujāhid*[52] does not fear poverty, starvation and even death. In order to make him afraid of privations and hardships it is necessary to expel the spirit of Muḥammad from his breast, and in order to destroy the distinctive personality, unity and rugged simplicity of the Arabs you ought to propagate atheism among them. Seize their spiritual heritage from the people of *Ḥaram* and eject Islam from his cradle. As you can see, religious pride is still alive among the hardy Afghans. For it, you will have to deal sternly with their theologians."

> Enmesh in politics the Brahmin—and
> From their ancient shrines the twice born expel.
> The man who raked with hunger fears not death-
> Muḥammad's spirit from his breast expel.
> Put Frankish thoughts into Arabia's mind—
> Islam from Yemen and Hejaz expel.
> Cure for the Afghan's pride of faith?
> The *Mulla* from his mountain and glen expel;
> Snatch from the people of *Ḥaram* their traditions—
> From Khutan's[53] meadows the musk deer expel.
> Iqbal's breath fans the tulip's flame red—
> Such a minstrel from the flower gardens expel.

Education can be the most appropriate means for the realisation of this end as it can infect the minds of Muslims with scepticism, sensuality and greed. Akbar Allahabadi has commented on the deadliness of the modern educational system in his typical style:

> Pharaoh would not have earned notoriety for infanticide,
> Had the idea of founding a college crossed his mind.

Iqbal feels that forces which have been hostile to Islamic interests have been largely successful. They have, to a great extent, accomplished what they wanted by undermining the religious consciousness of the Muslims and stifling the spirit of *Jihād* in them. Materialism is sweeping over the lands of Islam and Iqbal complains that during his travels round the Islamic world he saw the representatives of Abū Lahab[54] everywhere but those elevated with the spirit of Mohammed were extremely rare.

> In Ajamand Arabia I did wander,
> Bu Lahab in plenty, Muṣṭafā scarce.

He also feels that in the Arab countries the spiritual warmth for which the Arabs were famous has become extinct and in Persia the delicacy and refinement of thought and feeling is a thing of the past.

> On the battleground of life no Ghaznavi is left,
> Idols of the people of *Ḥaram* have for long been in wait.
> In the ardour of Arab's remembrance, in the music of Iranian's thought,
> Observations are not of Arabia, ideas not those of Iran.
> Not one Ḥusayn[55] in the caravan of Hejaz is found,
> Tresses of Tigris and Euphrates though are lustrous still.

Iqbal is saddened at the spectacle of decay and degeneration the Muslims present all over the world. He tries to arouse the torchbearers of Monotheism by telling them, "O inheritors of Islamic *Tawḥīd*! You possess neither the sweetness of speech which used to win hearts—nor the sternness of action by which you subdued adversaries. Once your glance used to be all conquering but now neither charm and appeal is present in you nor spirit and fervour."

> O inheritor of *Lā Ilāh!* In you is left,
> Neither the speech of loverhood nor sternness of action.
> Hearts in breasts once trembled at your glance,
> But in you the Qalandar's passion burns no more.

The poet, again, sorrowfully remarks that the arches and minarets of the mosques are yearning for the *Mu'min*'s genuflexion of love, and Egypt and Palestine are eager to hear the *Adhān*.

> Prostration at which the earth's soul trembled,
> Pulpit and arch for it are yearning.
> In Egypt and Palestine I did not hear,
> The *Adhān* that gave the mountain the creeps.

Sometimes, even an optimist like Iqbal sadly observes:
> Love's fire has died out. Darkness is complete,
> A heap of ashes, not a Muslim is he!
> Pearl of life in thy ocean does not exist,
> I looked for it in every wave and shell.

Sometimes in his anxiety to find an explanation for the melancholy state of affairs Iqbal concludes that as the spark of love has died out in the hearts of Muslims, and the blood of life has frozen in their veins they are no better than living corpses. They have become confused and have turned against one another.
> The madness of love is no more,
> The blood runs in Muslim's veins no more,
> Their prayer-ranks broken, hearts distracted, worship jaded,
> Because their inner passion is no more.

In spite of this, Iqbal believes that the process of regeneration has started in the Islamic World. In the poem, *Tulu-i-Islam* ("Dawn of Islam") he optimistically remarks that the paleness of the stars denotes that the end of the night is near. He is confident that the trials and hardships, rebuffs and setbacks will revive the religious spirit of the Muslims and they will become more loyal and faithful. They have already started to challenge the Western Civilisation, the significance of which cannot be explained but only felt.
> The faint light of stars tells the daybreak is near,
> The sun has risen, gone beyond the period of heavy slumber.
> In the East's chill veins life-blood flows again,
> Avicena and Farābī, this mystery cannot explain.
> The tempest of West has made the Muslim true in faith,
> In the tumult of sea pearl's fulfilment lies.
> To *Mu'min* from the Almighty is again to be granted,
> The dignity of Turk, the intellect of Indian, the eloquence of Arab.

The Muslims are a restless people. If they are sunk in a state of lethargy today it does not mean that they will always be like that.
> Restlessness from mercury can never depart.

The Muslim is the spokesman of Allah and is imperishable because he is the last message of God. He is the custodian of "all things" and his nature is the trustee of the boundless possibilities of life. Islam and life are the two names of the same reality. The resurgence of Muslims is pre-ordained.

> Boundless is thy knowledge, illimitable thy love,
> Thou art the choicest note in nature's harp.

In spite of all the disheartening circumstances Iqbal's faith in the latent potentialities of the Muslim *Millet* is undying.

> Of his desolate sowing-field Iqbal shall not despair,
> A little rain and the soil is most fertile, O Saqi!

He is convinced that the Western Civilisation has had its day. It can make no further contribution to the happiness of mankind and is already on the way to meet its end.

> In neither Asia, nor Europe life's struggle is on,
> Here it is Ego's death, there the death of conscience.
> Urge for revolution in the hearts is mounting,
> The end of the old world is haply near.

The foundations of the old world, on which the gamblers of the West have staked their existence, are crumbling and on its ruins a new world is going to be built. Iqbal asserts that only the builders of the House of Kaʿba and inheritors of the legacy of Abraham and Muḥammad (Peace of Allah be upon them) can be architects of the New World. He calls upon the Muslims to get ready for the task and appeals to them in the name of Allah. He draws attention to the dreadful plight of the world and speaks to them of the mischief and corruption that has been prevalent everywhere since the rise of Europe. The earth, which had been proclaimed to be as sacred as a mosque and on which God was to be remembered, has been turned into an alehouse, a gambling den, a lair of wild beasts and a hideout of robbers. Time has come for the architects of *Ḥaram* and the carriers of the divine message of Islam to resume the leadership of mankind, eradicate the

viciousness and injustice that has spread.
> You are the true guardian of the eternal rule,
> You are the left hand and right of the possessor of the world;
> O creature of clay! You are time and you are space,
> Drink the wine of faith and from doubt's prison rise;
> Out of heavy sleep, heavy sleep arise!
> Out of slumber deep arise!
> Against Europe I cry mercy and against the attraction of the West,
> Woe for Europe and her tyranny and her charm;
> Europe's hordes have laid the world waster,
> Architect of the *Haram* for rebuilding the world awake;
> Out of heavy sleep, heavy sleep arise!
> Out of slumber deep arise!

CHAPTER TEN

TO THE ARAB LANDS

In one of his selected poems, Iqbal expresses great love and admiration for the Arab countries. He alludes to the distinction they enjoy of defending the cause of Islam and of coming to the rescue of mankind at a time when it is immersed in ignorance.

From the start, Iqbal remembers the Arab through whose efforts the path of deliverance and progress was opened for humanity. He gives free rein to his feelings and an atmosphere of intense sincerity and exaltation is at once created.

> O Arab, for those deserts eternity has been ordained! O mighty race from which the world, for the first time, heard the thundering proclamation that the tyrannical order of Caesar and Chosroes had come to an end: To which community the Book of Books, the fadeless Quran, was first revealed? Whom did the Almighty trust with the secret of Monotheism? Who removed the fictitious deities from the pedestal of Divinity? In whose land was the torch of Guidance lighted that illumined the world? Can the name of anyone besides you be taken in reply to these questions? Knowledge and wisdom, piety and virtue are your gifts to mankind. And all this is the living miracle of the unlettered Prophet who transformed the arid desert into a blooming garden from which the breeze of freedom and equality blew and springs of culture and civilisation flowed to the far-flung regions of the earth. The body of the Arab was without a soul, the heart and the indwelling ego were granted to him; the dust of obscurity and ignorance fell away from his

face and he became known to the world. Arts were promoted, sciences were encouraged and the tree of civilisation sent forth new blossoms. From among the holy Apostle's servant arose mighty conquerors, peerless leaders and whole-souled divines to play a decisive role in the struggle between truth and iniquity. The Prophet gave to the world God-fearing crusaders who were horsemen by day and ascetics in the night, who gave the *Adhān* under the shadow of swords and offered *Namaz* in the thick of battle. The scimitar of the lofty-minded soldier, Ṣalāḥuddīn, and the glance of the glorious ascetic, Busṭāmī, held the guarantee of success in both the worlds.

Heart and mind, soul and intellect come together under the comprehensiveness of his message. The mystical insight of Rūmī and the intellectualism of Rāzī are merged into one another. Knowledge and wisdom, faith and law, government and administration are indebted to him. The Taj and the Al-Hamara are the resplendent gifts of the illustrious community of his followers to posterity. The splendid Islamic Civilisation is an external manifestation of the Prophet's keen ascetic sense. Even men of exceptional virtue and holiness cannot form an idea of his inner beauty. Before the advent of the Prophet, the "Mercy to the Worlds," man was a mere handful of dust. His Apostleship endowed him with faith and earnestness and knowledge and self-awareness. May thy lands, thy desert and wilderness, last till the crack of doom,

> Who did the end of Caesar and Chosroes proclaim?
> Who taught the secret of *Lā Ilāh?*
> Where was the lamp at first lighted?
> Touched by the breath of the Unlettered One,
> The sands of Arabia began to throw up tulips,
> Freedom under his protection has been reared,
> The "today" of nations from his "yesterday " is.
> He put heart into the body of man,

And from his face the veil he lifted.

> In the thick battle the majesty of *Adhān,*
> The recitation of *al-Ṣaffāt*[56] at the point of sword.
> The scimitar of Ayyūbī, the glance of Bayazīd,

Key to the treasures of this world and the next.
Ecstasy of heart and mind from the same wine-cup,
Fusion of Rūmī's devotion and Rāzī's thought,
Knowledge and wisdom, faith and law, government and politics,
Hearts in breasts devoid of peace.
Al-Hamara and Taj of breath-taking beauty,
To which even the angels pay tribute;
These, too, a fragment of his priceless bequest,
Of his countless glimpses only a glimpse.
His exterior these enthralling sights,
Of his interior even the knowing unaware.

Before the sacred Prophet, the Arabs scarcely deserved to be called a civilised people. There was no order or discipline among them and they revelled in anarchy and lawlessness. With little to choose between them and the quadrupeds, their understanding of life did not extend beyond eating and drinking. Though their sword shone brilliantly it lacked the edge. Before the dawn of Islam, the Arabs grazed the camels but, on coming under its influence, over-ran the world and held a large part of it under their sway. The East and the West began to resound with *Takbīr*.

Truth made thee sharper than sword,
Camel-drivers became the riders of destiny.
Nations have stolen a march on thee,
Thou realised no the worth of thy desert.
From one community thou split into several,
With thine own hands thou hast destroyed unity.
Whoever broke the bond of Ego perished,
Whoever fell into line with others was lost.

After praising the Islamic valour and the virility of the Arabs and their magnificent spirit of self-surrender it makes Iqbal sad to observe that they have lapsed into insipidity. Disagreements have taken the place of unity and enterprise. With profound anguish he addresses these words to them:

The whole world is grieving over your apathy and listlessness.

Other nations have forged ahead but you did not appreciate the worth of your desert and neglected its message. You were a single community but have now got divided into numerous nations. You were the "Party of Allah" but today there is no limit to factionalism in your ranks. Don't you know that he who disregards his Individuality and depends on others for help is destroyed and he who abandons his fortress and takes refuge with the enemy suffers humiliation? The Arabs are their own foremen. They have been unjust to themselves and caused pain to the spirit of the Prophet.

> What thou hast done to thyself none else did,
> Thou hast caused pain to the spirit of the Prophet.
> Ignorant of the witchery of the Frank,
> Behold the mischief hidden in his sleeve!
> By his diplomacy all nations prostrate,
> Unity of the Arabs crushed to pieces.
> As long as they are caught in his vicious trap,
> The Arabs shall not enjoy a moment's peace.

The poet's heart bleeds at the simplicity of the Arabs who still look to the West for sympathy and help. "O dupes!" he calls out to them, "Wake up! You trust the West and know nothing of its intentions. You do not realise how many nations have fallen prey to its artfulness. Don't you see that it has ruined your unity and divided you into a dozen states, perpetually falling out with each other?" Iqbal's optimism, then, reasserts itself and he ends his complaint and warning on a note of faith and hope. "Make use of the intellect God has given you," he advises them. "Turn the dying spark into a blazing flame. Produce the spirit of ʿUmar ibn al-Khaṭṭāb within you and know that the true fountainhead of strength is faith, which is the real asset of a Muslim in life. O dwellers of the desert! So long as your hearts are the trustees of Divine secrets you are the custodians of faith and sentinels of the world. Your inner self is the criterion of good and evil and you are genuine inheritors of the earth. When your star will rise in the East all other lights will fade."

O men of insight, look at the contemporary world,
Recreate within thyself the spirit of 'Umar. All strength is from faith,
And faith is conviction, resoluteness, and sincerity.
So long as thy conscience is Nature's confidant,
Man of desert is world's sentinel.
Thy unspoilt nature, the criterion of good and evil,
With thy appearance, a thousand stars fade.
Modern Age a creature of thy times,
Its ecstasy is from thy red wine.
Thou hast been the revealer of its mysteries,
And functioned as then first architect.
Since the West adopted it as a child,
It became courtesan without honour and shame.
Apparently sweet and loveable though,
It is crooked, faithless and impudent.
Bring the imperfect to perfection, O desert dweller!
And cast time into thine own mould.

Iqbal says, "The surroundings of the desert may be narrow and stifling but if you develop your individuality the horizons of your existence will widen beyond measure; you will become faster than the wind and no one will be able to stand up to you in the arena of life."

With a heavy heart he asks the Arabs, "Whoever has pushed you behind in the race of life in the Modern Age is the fruit of your endeavours. The day the reins of the world passed from your hands into those of the West, humanity lost its distinction, and hypocrisy and indifference to religion became its creed. O desert dweller! Realise your worth and significance, arrest the march of time, turn the tide of history and lead the caravan of mankind to its lofty goal and high destination."

Go past wilderness and habitation, hill and dale,
Pitch thy tent within thy being;
Develop thy personality stronger than blast,
Thrust thy camel into the field of strife;
Intellect of the West sword in hand,

> Bent like hell on slaughter of man!
> Glory of the daystar in the palm of thy hand;
> Trustee of the wealth of faith and civilisation,
> Bring the 'luminous hand' out of thy sleeve.

Iqbal addressed the spirit of the Prophet and grieves at the inertia and degradation of Muslims. "Islam has become a stranger in its own home," he says. "Confusion has set in among your followers and their solidarity has gone to wrack and ruin. Where are they to go? What should they do? The Arabian Sea has lost its tumult and the Arabs their passion. Who is there now to bring solace to me and to apply balm to the wounds of my heart? In the long and tedious journey of life the *Hadi Khwan*[57] of thy Ummah is disturbed and distressed. The destination is nowhere in sight. For the sake of God, take pity on the woeful state of thy followers and come to their rescue."

> The *Millet*[58] is in shambles, into disorder it has been thrown,
> Tell us yourself, O Prophet, which way should your faithful turn?
> Now no more the Arabian Sea with love of tumult foams,
> Which way should the tempest concealed within me turn?
> Though there is no caravan left, no camel, no provision here
> From this rocky desert which way shall Hadi Khwan turn?
> Now at last, oh spirit of Muḥammad, unravel this knot,
> Which way should the guardian of Divine verses turn?

It is most hurtful to Iqbal that in spite of repeated experiences, the Muslims should still regard the Western powers as friendly and sympathetic and even look up to them for the solution to their problems, especially that of Palestine. He remarks, "I know that the flame of life that once burnt so brightly among the Arabs is even now alive and can burst forth at any time. I am also convinced that the solution to their difficulties does not lie with London or Geneva but in the development of their Ego." In the end, he dares to address these forceful words to the leaders of the Arab World:

To the Arab Lands

O People of Arabia! You were the first to appreciate the reality of Faith and you also know that loyalty to the sacred Prophet demands a complete break with Abū Lahab. Islam and apostasy are utterly opposed to each other. In the same way, Islam is intolerant of nationalism, as of all other materialistic ideologies, and the Islamic World is not the name of certain territories, but signifies whole-hearted devotion to the holy Prophet and unqualified dedication to the Islamic faith.

May this Indian apostate also speak—
If it be not disrespectful to Arab leaders?
To which community was the truth first revealed:
Allegiance to Muḥammad turning away from Bu Lahab is?
Frontiers and territories do not the Arab World make,
Its existence from Muḥammad of Arabia is!

CHAPTER ELEVEN

THE MOSQUE OF CORDOBA

In 1932, Iqbal visited Spain and also went to see the Mosque of Cordoba. It was not an ordinary sightseeing trip by a tourist interested in ancient monuments but a pilgrimage to an outstanding symbol of faith by a faithful Believer and a warm-hearted poet. It was a pilgrimage of love and loyalty by a celebrated Muslim to pay homage to the spiritual legacy of Abdul Rahman el-Dakhil and his companions.

Iqbal was greatly moved by the magnificence and solemnity of the Mosque and the deep emotional responses its awe-inspiring sight evoked in him found expression in the immortal poem called *Masjid-i-Qartaba* ("The Mosque of Cordoba"). Iqbal saw it as a cultural landmark of Islam and in its architecture and engravings he saw a moving portrait of the Believer's moral excellence and aesthetic refinement as well his high-mindedness, sincerity, piety and devotion.

The Mosque reminded Iqbal of its builders and their keen appreciation of artistic beauty, and of the noble ideas and appreciation, call and message, they upheld in life and propagated in the world. Its tall, stately minarets revived the memory of the spellbinding *Adhān* that once used to rise from them and which people heard every day at the beginning and the end of the stresses of life. The *Adhān* is a symbol of the unity and solidarity of the Muslim *Millet*. The call it gives and the message it conveys may, indeed, be described as the National Anthem of Muslims and it is unique to their community. At one time the soul of the universe trembled and the foundations of the citadels of falsehood shook at the sound of it.

It was the Islamic *Adhān* that announced the dawn of a new morning and dispelled the gloom that had enveloped the world in the sixth century AD. Iqbal recalls the Divine message and the celestial guidance the *Adhān*s used to carry to the four corners of the world and the depth and intensity of their significance. The more he ponders over it the more is he convinced that the *Millet* which is endowed with this eternal call and lives according to this everlasting message is also imperishable.

The beautiful a scene of such a wonderful Mosque and historical monument (whose pulpit for centuries had remained deprived of enormous sermons, courtyard and arches of genuflexion and minarets of *Adhān*) touched the soul of his being and opened the unhealed wounds. His feelings were stirred with faith and awareness, but were also mingled with those of pain, disappointment, grief and anguish that began to rise in him. It was in these circumstances that the enthralling poem, *Masjid-i-Qartaba*, was conceived, part of which was written in Cordoba itself and the rest then completed during his stay in Spain.

The poem is an unsurpassed masterpiece of poetic inspiration and artistic expression. In it Iqbal says that the material world is not everlasting. It is transitory, and, with it, all the wonders of art and architecture, historical buildings and ancient monuments are heading towards ruin and destruction. However, constructions like the Mosque of Cordoba are an exception since they have been touched by the messianic hand of a man of God and a devoted Believer and thus shine with the radiance of his love.

Love is the everlasting essence of life and a feeling and action that stands up to the march of time. It transcends time and space and its wondrous possibilities are beyond human comprehension. There are states and stages of love that are not known to anyone.

The Mosque of Cordoba

The radiance of love is common to all Divine Apostleships and sacred teachings.

The entire colour, radiance, joy and fragrance of the universe stems from love. It purifies the Believer and reveals itself, sometimes in the form of a preacher from the pulpit and sometimes as a philosopher and conqueror. It is multifaceted and restless being at the same time, an eternal wayfarer and a perpetual traveller. Love fills the world with delight and from it come the sentiments of activity, movement, ardour and enthusiasm.

> Chain of days and nights—artificer of all events
> Chain of days and nights—fountain of life and death!
> Chain of days and nights—thread of two-coloured silk
> Of which the Being makes the robe of His Attributes!
> Chain of days and nights-sigh of eternity's music
> Where He of all possibility sounds the height and depth!
> Thee it puts to test and me it puts to test,
> Day and night in procession, testers of this entire world.
> If thou art of less value and I am of less value,
> Find in death our reward and in dissolution our wage.
> Of your day and night what other meaning but this—
> One long current of time, devoid of dawn and sunset
> All those masterpieces of art, transitory and impermanent;
> All in this world is of sand; all in this world is of sand!
> Death the beginning and end, death to the visible and hidden;
> New be the pattern or old, its final halting-place is death.
> Yet in this design of things, something unending endures,
> Wrought by some man of God into perfection's mould;
> Some high moral whose work shines with the light of love,
> Love is the essence of life, death to which is forbidden.
> Long current of Time, strong and swift though it is,
> Love itself is a tide, stemming all opposite waves;
> In the almanac of Love, apart from the present time,
> Other ages exist, ages, which have no name.
> Love is the breath of Gabriel. Love is the Prophet's heart,
> Love the envoy of God; Love the utterance of God;
> Under the ecstasy of Love our mortal clay is bright,
> Love is an unripe wine; Love is a cup for the noble.

> Love is the legist of *Ḥaram*; Love is the commander of hosts,
> Love is the son of travel, countless its habitations;
> Love is the plectrum that plucks songs from the chords of life,
> Love is the brightness of life. Love is the fire of life.

After this long prologue Iqbal turns to the Mosque and addresses these words to it:

> O Mosque of Cordoba! For thy existence and thy glory thou art indebted to love, to the tender passion that is immortal. In this way, thou too art eternal. Philosophy, art, and poetry, or any other form of literary or artistic activity, is shallow and insincere if it is not fed with the blood of the heart. It is no more than an empty structure of word and sound, paint and oil, or brick and stone, possessing neither beauty, nor life, nor freshness. Works of art, of whatever excellence they may be, cannot endure without the intensity of inner passion, depth of love and profundity of earnestness. It is love, which distinguishes man from sculpted figure. When a drop of love's warm blood falls upon a piece of marble it turns into a beating heart and if even a man's heart is destitute of love it is a slab of stone. O magnificent Mosque! In love and eagerness we both are alike. There is a mystical affinity between you and me. Man, in his creation, is a handful of dust but his heart is the envy of the ninth heaven. The human heart is also lit up with the lustre of Divinity and the joy of Presence: Angels, indeed, are famous for unending genuflexion but the warmth and delight of human prostration has not been granted to them.

Referring to his Indian and Brahmin origin Iqbal says:

> Look at the fervour and earnestness of this Indian infidel! He was born and brought up in the home of infidelity but his lips and heart are constantly engaged in prayer and invocation, benediction and salutation. On meeting you in this strange land he has become a picture of intentness and devotion. There obtains a complete uniformity and an understanding between your soul and mine!

> Oh shrine of Cordoba, thou owest existence to love,
> Deathless in all its being, stranger to Past and Present.
> Colour or brick and stone, speech or music and song,

The Mosque of Cordoba

Only the heart's warm blood feeds the craftsman's design;
One drop of heart's blood lends marble a beating heart,
Out of the heart's blood flow out warmth, music and mirth.
Thine the soul-quickening air, mine the soul-quickening verse,
From thee the pervasion of men's hearts, from me the opening of men's' hearts.
Inferior to the Heaven of Heavens, by no means the human breast is,
Handful of dust though it be, hemmed in the azure sky.
What is prostration be the lot of the heavenly host?
Warmth and depth of prostration they do not ever feel.
I, a heathen of Ind, behold my fervour and my ardour,
Ṣalāt[59] and Durood fill my soul; Ṣalāt and Durood are on my lips!
Fervently sounds my voice; ardently sounds my lute,
Allāh Hu,[60] like a song, thrilling through every vein!

Whilst observing this wonderful architecture, Iqbal is reminded of the real Muslim, the true Believer, whom only Islam can produce.

In Iqbal's view, the totality of appearance and effectiveness of the Mosque of Cordoba is a material manifestation of the *Mu'min*. In its beauty and elegance, height and width, gracefulness and solidity, fineness and strength it is his exact replica. Its imposing pillars remind Iqbal of the oases of Arabia and in its balconies and latticed windows he sees the indication of heaven. He regards its towering minarets to be the descending points of Divine mercy and the halting places of the angels. Overcome with emotion he cries out: "The Muslim is imperishable, he shall not die, because he is the bearer of the message of Abraham and Moses and of all the Divine Apostles."

Iqbal declares that the Mosque of Cordoba is a true symbol of the beliefs, thoughts and aspirations of the Muslim *Millet*. Just as the Muslim *Millet* is free from all the narrow and unnatural concepts of race and nationality, the Mosque, too, represents a marvellous synthesis of Arab and Persian cultures and typifies a remarkable supra-national fraternity. The Muslim is above territorial limitations and his world is boundless, for the beauty and warmth of his message is all pervading. The Tigris and the Euphrates of Iraq, the Ganges and the Jumma of India, the Danube of Europe and the Nile of Egypt all belong to him. His achievements are unequalled in history for it was the Muslim *Millet* that ushered in the new age.

Members of the Islamic *Millet* inspire compassion and respect for others, thus becoming the true specimens of faith and brotherhood. The *Mu'min* is well tempered, content in his heart and persevering in action. Even on the battlefield he is the upholder of Monotheism and Apostleship and sets out on the path of piety and righteousness. In the struggle between truth and falsehood faith is his weapon and reliance upon God his armour.

> Thou, in beauty and dignity, man of God's witness,
> He is beautiful and dignified; thou art beautiful and dignified.
> Firm are thy foundations; numberless are thy pillars,
> Soaring like ranks of palms over the Syrian Desert.
> Light of the Valley of Peace gleams on thy walls and roof,
> On thy minaret's height Gabriel stands in glory.
> The Muslim shall not perish for by his *Adhān*,
> The secret of Moses and Abraham is revealed.
> Limitless in his world, boundless his long horizon,
> Tigris and Danube and Nile but a wave in his sea.
> His times are wondrous; his legends are strange,
> To the ages outworn he gave the command to depart.
> Saqi of men of taste, horseman of the realm of desire,
> Pure and unmixed his wine, tempered and glittering his steel.
> Warrior armed in the mail of *Lā Ilāh*,
> Under the shadow of swords succoured by *Lā Ilāh*.

The poet, again, says to the Mosque:

You are the interpretation of the *Mu'min*'s dream in the world, the exposition of his high-mindedness and the exemplification of his soul in brick and mortar. The hand of the *Mu'min*, in power and dominance, in the dispersal of difficulties and the fulfilment of needs, is the Hand of God and an instrument of Providence. Apparently, he is born of clay but in reality, he has the nature of Light. There is the reflection of Divine Attributes in his being. He is indifferent to the allurements of the World. His desires are few, but his aims are high. He is the embodiment of grace and strength, love and sternness. He is gentle of speech, but warm in quest. In peace he is soft like silk, but in war hard as steel. The faith of the Believer is the pivot on which the world turns. His existence is the essence of creation and all the rest an illusion. In him thought and intellect, faith and love find their highest expression. Strength and felicity in life and beauty and elegance in the world owe their presence to him. He is the end and object of the pilgrimage of love and the heart and soul of the universe.

> Behold in thy stones are all the Believer's secrets,
> Fire of passionate days, rapture of melting nights.
> High is his station and great are his thoughts,
> Ecstasy, burning desire, self-abasement and pride.
> The hand of the *Mu'min* is the hand of Allah—
> Dominant, resourceful, creative, ensuring success.
> Fashioned of dust and light, slave with the Master's attributes,
> His heart is indifferent to the riches of the worlds.
> His earthly hopes are few; his aims are high,
> Courtesy is his mien, gaining all hearts with his glance;
> He is soft of speech but fierce in the hour of pursuit,
> In war and peace pure in thought and in act,
> The point of God's great compass the Believer's firm faith,
> All this universe else-shadow, illusion, deceit.
> He is the goal of love; he is the end of Love,
> He, in the circle of the firmament, sets all spirits aglow.

Iqbal goes on to pay a tribute of never-fading charm to the Mosque. "Thou art the Makkah of the seekers of Art," he says, "the place of pilgrimage for the devotee of love and the symbol of the glory of Islam. Thanks to thee, the soil of Cordoba is vying for sacredness and elevation with the heavens. If anything can compare with thee it is the heart of the true Believer." Here

Iqbal loses control of his feelings. He looks at the distant past and centuries roll back in his imagination. He begins to live in the period of Muslim ascendancy in Spain. Combining romanticism with classicism he asks, "Where are the Moorish horsemen, the men of virtue, the embodiments of faith and the champions of truth? Where has their unrelenting caravan stopped? Where have the Arab rulers, the precursors of European Renaissance, gone whose government was another name for social justice and public welfare?"

Iqbal feels that Spain is still affected by the Arabs. Oriental charm, hospitality and sincerity can even now be seen among its people. Its air is filled with the scent of Najd and Yemen and the music of Iraq and Arabia is heard in its atmosphere.

> Shrine of the seekers of art! Glory of the manifest Faith!
> Thou Andalusia's soil sacred as Makkah hast made.
> If there is underneath the sky beauty equal to thine,
> Nowhere shall it be found, but in the Muslim's heart.
> Ah, those champions of Right, those fearless horsemen of Arabia,
> Bearers of high morality, knights of the truth and faith!
> By their rule this strange secret to all was revealed,
> Men of pure hearts hold sway, not to enslave but to serve.
> East and West by their eyes gained instruction,
> In the darkness of Europe their minds showed the path.
> Even today Andalusia, rich with their blood, is seen,
> Gay and friendly of heart, simple and bright of face;
> Even today in this land, eyes like the soft gazelle's,
> Dart their glances, giving pleasure to the hearts;
> Even today in its breeze fragrance of Yemen endures,
> Even today in its songs echoes subsist of Hejaz.

In spite of these sorrowful recollections, Iqbal's imagination is fired with the desire for change. He says that though the land of Andalusia enjoys the high position of the heavens, it has not heard the *Adhān* and it is in need of the Islamic revolution. Martin Luther's Protestant Reformation in Germany not only led to the decline of Papal authority and the extinction of the domination of the Church but it also made its impact on language, literature and civilisation and paved the way for the cultural revival of Europe. The philosophy of Rousseau and Voltaire brought about the Revolution of France and ushered in the industrial era. Even conservative Italy had been showing signs of regeneration.

Against this background Iqbal yearns for an Islamic revolution. He believes that the revolutionary spirit of the Muslim is also uneasy but one does not know when it is going to assert itself. To Vudi-El-Kabir (Guadalquiver) he says, "On your bank a stranger is seeing the image of the future in the mirror of the past. Fascinating though the dream is, it is so intolerable to Europe that it cannot listen calmly to my plain-speaking."

Strife and revolt produce the destiny of nations. Those who watch their steps carefully and analyse their feelings and keep an eye on their mental processes are successful in life and make their mark in history. About art and thought, poetry and literature, Iqbal once again emphasises that a philosophy that is not written with the blood of the heart is no more than a mental exercise. The vital flame, the breath of life, is missing from it. Likewise, the greatest works of art fade away if the blood of the artist does not flow into them, and music that does not spring from the depths of the soul is transient and superficial. This is Iqbal's concept of art as well as of life.

> Thy land is like the heavens in the sight of the stars—
> For ages, alas, thy atmosphere has remained bereft of the Adhān.
> In what dale and glen, in what stage of the journey,
> Love's undaunted caravan now happens to be?
> Germany saw, long ago, Change and Revolution—
> Obliterating the old ways, sweeping away every trace,
> Holiness of pop fast became an erroneous word,
> Thought in its fragile boat launched on its dangerous course,
> The eye of France, also, has seen Revolution rage,
> That overturned the world the Westerners had known,

The Roman nation, old and tires with ancient traditions,
With the joy of rejuvenation discovered again her youth.
Now that tempest has seized even the soul of Islam,
A Divine secret it is whose meaning cannot be told by the tongue.
Watch! From the surface of this ocean what portents finally emerge,
What new turn the blue revolving dome takes!
Drowned in the twilight is the cloud in the mountain gorge,
The sun has left behind heaps of the rubies of Badakhshan.
Running water of Guadalquiver! On your bank is a stranger,
Lost in his thoughts, dreams of another age.
Behind the Destiny's curtain the New World is yet concealed,
But to mine eyes its dawn already stands unveiled.
Were I to lift the veil from the face of my thoughts,
Europe could not endure the burning heat of my songs.
Death, not life, is the life, in which no revolution takes place,
Strife and revolt are the sustenance of nations' souls.
Keen as a sword that nation is in the hand of Fate,
Which at every moment takes account of its works and deeds.
Works of creation are incomplete without the heart's warm blood,
Music is an immature frenzy without the heart's warm blood.

CHAPTER TWELVE

ARDOUR AND EAGERNESS

The year 1931 saw the *Motamar-i-Islami* (International Islamic Conference) in Jerusalem. On this morning, the air was refreshing, the surroundings were delightful, and the sun had just risen spreading its golden rays on all sides. Early dawn has always fascinated the poets and our poet and the ethereal beauty of the time and place captivated philosopher, Dr. Muhammad Iqbal, who had come from Europe to represent the Muslims of India at the *Motamar*. He saw everything around him eagerly and gave free reign to his imagination there.

The land of Palestine was full of clouds of various shades, from silver to dark and green mountains. The gentle drafts of the morning breeze, the sands and the lilies, cypresses and leaves of the date palms that had been washed by the overnight rain must have enchanted him. Glimpses of the rugged austerity of Arab life would have flashed through his mind. The blown out fire, the torn ropes of tents and the marks of broken camps would have reminded him of caravans that had gone past. He was so bewitched by the scenic beauty of this paradise on earth that he thought of settling down over there. The entire atmosphere of the birthplace of the prophets sparked a hope in him and stimulated his unrealised dreams. The intensity of feeling made him all too aware of his undying love for Islam and the Muslims. The favourite theme of Islamic revival pushed itself forward and Iqbal went through the same experience as has been related by an Arab poet in these lines of enduring beauty: "When I dismounted at the place as fresh as the dew and as fragrant as a garden, the beauty of the surroundings awoke certain desires in me and the centre of those desires were you."

Iqbal's imagination and creativity was stirred and he felt that the old and crumbling world was not fitted to receive his ideas. The old world had become rigid, conventionalised and narrow-minded and was only preoccupied with country, sex and nationality. In the face of shameful sensuality and self-indulgence Iqbal prayed for another Abraham to rise and break the new idols.

As the poet looks at the Islamic World he is appalled not only by its material backwardness but, also, intellectual insolvency. The Arabs have lost the strength of faith and the courage of conviction. Their souls have become dead and unresponsive-and the non-Arabs, too, have become fixed in their ideas.

The modern materialistic age is waiting for a revolutionary man of God that can play the role of the defender of Truth on an international scale and revive the memory of Imam Ḥusayn. The Muslim World is looking expectantly at the Arab World, and at Hejaz, the cradle of Islam, to raise the banner of revolt but no hopeful sign is visible.

Iqbal declares that the decline of Muslims is due to their lack of religious zeal and self-esteem. He argues that love should be one of the cornerstones of life and the foundations of belief should be fortified with sincerity. Unless the Muslims develop an emotional involvement with Islam it will remain a collection of soulless beliefs.

Love overcomes the known laws of nature and makes things possible that are outside of cause and effect. Sometimes it takes the form of the truthfulness of Khalīl, sometimes of the fortitude of Ḥusayn and sometimes of the courage and bravery of the hero of Badr and Ḥunayn.

Daybreak in the desert, feast for the heart and the eye,

Rivers of light from the fount of sun flowing;
Divine Beauty is on display, rent is the curtain of existence,
A loss for the eye-a thousand gains for the heart;
Purple bits in the air the night's cloud has left,
Mount Izam worth a multi-coloured sheet it has covered;
The breeze is pure, leaves of date-palms washed by rain,
Sands of Kazima soft as silk;
Fire is dead, broken the ropes of tents,
Who knows how many caravans have passed along?
Came the voice of Gabriel? "This is the place for you-
For those separated from the beloved it's eternal bliss!"
Poison for me is the wine of life, but who listens?
Old is the congregation of the world, new my ideas are!
On the battleground of life no Ghazni is left,
Idols of the people of *Ḥaram* have for long been in wait.
In the ardour of Arab's remembrance, in the music of Iranian's thought,
Observations are not of Arabia nor ideas those of Persia.
Not one Ḥusayn in the caravan of Hejaz is found,
Tresses of Tigris and Euphrates though are lustrous still.
Love is the prime mentor of the head and heart,
Without love Faith and Law concepts' idol-hall;
Truthfulness of Khalīl is love; fortitude of Ḥusayn is love,
In life's unrelenting battle, Badr and Ḥunayn are love.

Reverting to the theme of the perfect man Iqbal says that his existence is the foremost purpose of creation; he is the secret of *Be and it is!*, the lost Paradise and the stolen wealth which the soul of the world is trying hard to recover.

He is also distressed at the moral and spiritual bankruptcy and intellectual inactivity of the Islamic world. The quest of Knowledge, originality of thought, idealism and intentness are absent even from educational institutions and spiritual lodges.

The poet looks around for the flame of life that once imparted light and heat to the world and for the spark of belief and in the men of faith.

Iqbal is conscious of the worth and significance of his poetry and claims that his verses nourish and sustain the heart because they carry the message of faith and life from his warm heart.

> Thou art the hidden meaning of the verse of creation,
> Parties of hue and scent have gone out in thy search.
> Scholars of the seminary visionless and unambitious,
> Votaries of the tavern lacking in thirst, short of decanter.
> I, in my poem, traces of fire that used to be,
> My whole life a quest of the missing ones.
> Nourishment of the thorn and straw in the morning breeze,
> By my breath desire is sustained.
> My song is fed by the blood of my heart,
> In the string of the lyre flows minstrel's blood.
> Oh! Let there be no peace for the restless heart,
> Add a few more curls to thy lustrous hair.

The last part of the poem is devoted to prayer:

Thy radiance surrounds the universe. The world is a mere particle of Thy boundless desert and life a drop of the unfathomable sea of Thy Existence. By the touch of Thy Splendour the manifestation of the sun becomes possible in the atom and the presence of the ocean a drop of water. Lives and deeds of powerful kings and conquerors pale into nothingness before the display of Thy Might and the hearts of whole-souled men and benefactors of humanity are illumined with Thy sublimity. Thy love is the song-leader of my soul and the interpreter of my heart. Joy and spirituality of my worship is due to it. When my devotions are not blessed with Thy love they become the message of separation, not of union. Both love and intellect have been ordained to seek closeness unto Thee. Study and observation, curiosity and reflection, dignity and self-reliance have been allocated to the mind, and ardour and eagerness, disquietude and restlessness, joy and felicity to the heart. Light in the world is not because of the sun but a reflection of Thy Beauty.

Iqbal admits that long years of study and research alone could not fulfil him. The struggle between spirituality and materialism has been going on since the beginning of time and the conflict between truth and falsehood is eternal even within the history of Islam. Iqbal is reminded of the first encounter in which Abū Jahl,[61] Abū Lahab and their deputies propagated the creed materialism and the sacred Prophet and his Anṣārs[62] set out to uphold Truth. The task before the Arab and the Islamic World today is to make the choice between the two opposing forces.

> Thou art the Tablet and the Pen, Thy existence in the Book,
> The blue revolving dome a tiny bubble of Thy Sea,
> The world of water and clay bright by Thy presence,
> Thou upon the dust-particle bestowed the dawn of the sun.
> Power of Sanjar and Salim, a manifestation of Thy Might,
> Asceticism of Junayd and Bayazīd, Thy Beauty uncovered.
> Should Thy Love not be the leader of my *Namaz*,
> My Qiyām is mere farce, my Sujūd only a mask.
> Mind and heart—by Thine alluring glance are fulfilled,
> One got search and quest, the other unrest and turmoil.
> Dark and dingy is the world by the movement of the sun,
> Take off Thy veil and revive the drooping spirits of time.
> All my past days and nights are known to Thee,
> That horticulture was bare of fruit I never knew;
> The old battle in my soul has begun again,
> Love is all Muṣṭafā, intellect nothing but Bu Lahab.
> Sometimes with deception it works, sometimes with force,
> Strange is the beginning of Love; strange is its end!
> In the world of strife and revolt separation is better than union,
> In union the death of desire, in separation the joy of longing.
> At the time of union I dared not cast a glance,
> In search of a pretext though my insolent eyes were.
> Separation is the heat of desire; separation is the tumult of groan,
> Separation is the quest of tide; separation is the glory of the drop.

The poem *Zauq-o-Shauq* ("Ardour and Earnestness") is one of Iqbal's masterpieces. In form and substance it is very much like the *Masjid-i-Qartaba*. It contains an enchanting depiction of natural beauty and of the plain yet refreshing lifestyle of the Arabs. As the poem progresses, Iqbal touches on most of the themes that are characteristic to his poetry and philosophy. With a phenomenal keenness of perception and maturity of thought, he enters into the soul of countries and communities; and through a rare combination of poetical fluency and intellectual penetration, he analyses their distinguishing traits and capacity for good and evil. He not only knows the West intimately but is also acquainted with the inner urges and latent powers of the Orient—Arabia, Iran and Afghanistan. Apart from describing the scenic beauty of Palestine, Iqbal has woven into it the simple experience of everyday life like the blown out fire and the broken ropes of tents so admirably and emotionally that it does not fail to exercise a moving effect on the reader.

CHAPTER THIRTEEN

THE PROBLEM OF PALESTINE

Iqbal was intensely interested in the problem of Palestine and the deep anxiety he felt for the future of the Arabs never ceased to trouble him. We can obtain an idea of the uneasiness of his mind from his letters, especially those written to Miss Farquharson.

To Mr. Mohammad Ali Jinnah he once wrote, "The question of Palestine is agitating the minds of Indian Muslims. It may be possible for the Muslim League to render some service to the Palestinian Arabs. Personally, I am prepared to court imprisonment for a cause that concerns both India and the Muslims. The establishment of a Western outpost as the gateway of Asia can be dangerous for Islam as well as India."[63]

Similarly in a letter to Miss Farquharson he says, "The Jews have no claim over Palestine. They had voluntarily left it long before the occupation by the Arabs. Zionism is not a religious movement. Besides the fact that religious-minded Jews are not interested in it, the Palestine Report, itself, is clear on the point."[64]

In one way or another, Iqbal was associated with all the conferences that were held about it in India. He issued a forceful statement when the Muslims of Lahore met to protest against the Palestine Report which read, "I am as much distressed at the injustice done to the Arabs as anyone can be who is in touch with the situation in the Middle East. The problem gives an opportunity to the Muslims to declare unequivocally that what the British statesmen are trying to solve does not concern Palestine alone, but will have wide repercussions in the entire Islamic World. Historically, Palestine is wholly a Muslim problem. The Jewish problem had ceased to exist in Palestine thirteen hundred years ago, before the entry of ʿUmar into Jerusalem. The Jews were never forcibly expelled from it. According to Prof. Hocking they had themselves freely decided to migrate to other lands and a major portion of their Scriptures was compiled outside Palestine. It was never a Christian problem also. Modern historical researches have cast a doubt even on the existence of Peter the Hermit."[65]

At the termination of World War I, the wrath of the victorious Allied Powers fell upon the Islamic World. The Ottoman Empire broke into fragments and the Allies set about dividing it amongst themselves. Russia annexed the eastern part of Turkey, and the Western provinces like Hungary, Bulgaria, Yugoslavia and Albania were made independent. Iran and Syria were taken over by France as Protectorates while Iraq and Egypt passed into the hands of the British. Palestine had an international significance and so Britain assumed its trusteeship. Iqbal throws light on these despicable deals and exposes the plan of the Western Imperialists who devour the weaker nations and then show hypocritical grief over their misfortune.

> Blessed be thy kind heart that for Divine Recompense,
> Thou attended the funeral service of thy own victim.

The West calls it "white man's burden," trusteeship and progress but, in truth, it is pure exploitation.

> Iqbal does not doubt Europe's nobility,
> Of every oppressed nation she is the buyer;
> But my heart burns for Syria, Palestine,
> And this hard riddle of fate none can lay bare;
> Freed from Turkey's "savage grasp," they pine,
> Poor wretches! Now in civilisation's snare.

The League of Nations had done little to mitigate the sufferings of Arabs and Asians. It had failed to bring about an improvement primarily because the Jews and the Western nations who lost no opportunity to use it for their selfish ends dominated it. Iqbal condemns it as the "kept woman of the old man of Europe" and the "association of shroud-lifters."

> An association thy have formed for the division of graves.

Iqbal foresees the consequences of the growing influence of the Jews in the political and the economic life of the West and fears that sooner or later it will give in to their demands.

> Jewish usurers have for long been in wait,
> Before whose cunning lion's strength is not anything.
> Like ripened fruit the West is going to fall,
> Let's see in whose lap it drops.

In another poem, *Europe Aur Yuhud* ("Europe and the Jews"), he expresses the same sentiment.

> Sick before its prime, this Civilisation is at its last grasp,
> And the sole trustees of Christendom Jews are likely to be.

After the Arab-Israel War of June 1967, the Jews and their supporters declared that since the Arabs unjustly expelled them from their homeland no one could blame them from trying to reoccupy it by force. Palestine was the Promised Land to which the Jews were bound to return one day or the other.

Iqbal pointed out that the Jews had themselves decided to move out of Palestine willingly and long before the Arab occupation. Moreover, he argued that if the principle advanced by the Jews and their Western patrons was accepted and Palestine was handed over to the Zionists what could prevent the Arabs from laying claim to Sicily, Spain and the other European lands that were once in their possession? Or, coupled by the same logic, the Red Indians did not assert their right over America and the Aryans of India did not demand that Iran and Russia should be returned to them. Iqbal thought that it was a ridiculous distortion of history and maintained that if the Jews must be provided with a home it should be in Germany from where they had been banished.

> If the Jew claims the soil of Palestine,
> Why has the Arab race no right to Spain?
> The aim of British Imperialism is different,
> It is not a matter of history, honey or dates.

Iqbal wants to arm the Palestinian Arabs with the weapons of faith and self-awareness. He is convinced that it is only through reliance upon God and upon themselves that they can regain freedom. International forums will not allow them to gain anything.

> I know that in your being burns the fire,
> Whose heat to this day the world remembers;
> Your balm lies neither in London nor Geneva,
> The Jewish grasp is tight on Europe's throat.
> But nations throw off bondage, it is told,
> By cultivating Selfhood and zest for living.

CHAPTER FOURTEEN

IN AFGHANISTAN

In 1933, Iqbal was invited to Afghanistan by King Nadir Shah. He also visited Ghazni, the capital of Mahmud Ghaznavi, and visited the tomb of *Sunai*[66] the philosopher, whom he regarded as his mentor, next only to Maulana Rūmī. It proved to be a unique experience and the verses he wrote there are richly illustrative of his exceptional artistic and intellectual ability. In them he has directed his attention at the contemporary world as a creator of values and a judge of his environment.

Iqbal expresses pain and discontent at the "languor and tardiness of the fellow-travellers" and at the "narrowness and triviality of the world" which has turned out to be a "straitjacket" for his high-soaring ideas. He even finds that the hills, valleys, forests and deserts are too narrow to contain the stirrings of his heart and says that the whole system of material objects and the space in which these exist cannot contain the sentiments of those blessed by God with vision and love. The enlightened souls of Men of God, thus, feel compelled to cut themselves free from the material world and follow an alternative path. Iqbal calls it the "secret of *Tawḥīd*" which opens the door of awareness of God

in the Believers and they begin to see the glimpses of the other world in their earthly existence.

> The vastness of Nature cannot harbour the wild stirrings,
> Oh my madness! Wrong, perhaps, was thy estimate of the wilderness,
> The strong Self can burst through the enchantments of sense,

Tawḥīd[67] it was which neither you nor I could know.

The traditional rivalry between *Ṭarīqah* (Mysticism) and *Sharīʿah* (strict obseverance of the Divine Law) is more imaginary than real. There is no contradiction between knowledge and intuition and faith and love. It is only the false reasoning of the claimants to *Sharīʿah* and *Ḥaqīqah* (Reality) that makes them suspicious about love. Iqbal also contends that the real thing for the devotees of *Sharīʿah* and *Ḥaqīqah* is supreme indifference to the rewards the world has to offer. This is their glory and they can only be content when they turning their backs upon the wealthy and renowned. As he is reminded of the devotees' glowing feats of endurance and heroism; he feels like reproaching even Archangel Gabriel and observes that even the holy spirits cannot emulate the example of man when it comes to love and submission.

> Rivalry between Reason and Vision is the fallacy of the pulpit,
> Which regards the scaffold of Ḥallāj[68] its permanent foe.
> If there is any shield to guard the pure ones of the Lord,
> In thraldom or dominion, it is the scorn of this world's show.
> Try not, Oh Gabriel, to emulate my passion and ecstasy,
> For ease-loving angels Dhikr,[69] Tasbīḥ[70] and Ṭawāf[71] are best.

The poet is critical of both the East and the West. He examines them closely, studying their merits and faults and analyses their problems and difficulties. He then comes to the conclusion that the East is not lacking in potential but its problem is that proper guidance and leadership is not available to it while the West is intoxicated with power, and the excessive indulgence in material pleasures has produced a state of ennui in it. He recalls the great men of the East who had challenged the might of Chosroes and before whose supreme contentment powerful kings and potentates took fright. The very existence of these marvellous humans symbolised the triumph of truth over falsehood. Iqbal is saddened at the pitiful state of the Arab World and his sense of pride is stirred as he witnesses the treachery, ineptitude and debauchery of its rulers. He laments that these dishonourable men can even sell away the blank of Abū Dharr, the habit of Owais and the mantle of Zahra and allow the holy places of Islam to be desecrated by non-Muslims.

He compares the present plight of the Arab countries and the growing influence of the West in them with the Day of Judgement and recites the verse Sunai wrote at the time of Tartar invasion, saying that while the Chinese and Turkish hordes had advanced to the House of Kaʿba the people of the Ḥaram were fast asleep.

> I have seen many a wine-shop of the East and West,
> Here no Saqi fills the cup, there in the wine no lambent glow,
> In Iran they are no more, nor in Turan,
> Bondsmen whose contentment was the death of Shah and Caesar.
> Hucksters rule the Ḥaram who sell for profit,
> The blanket of Abū Dharr, habit of Owais and Zahra's mantle.
> Before the Lord, Raphael against me complained, "This rash creature may not bring the Day of Wrath before its hour!" "Is it less terrible," came the Voice, "than Judgement Day, that while the Chinese have donned the pilgrim's robe, the Makkan is asleep in Batha?"[72]

Iqbal analyses the characteristics of the Western civilisation and arrives at the opinion that balance and stability cannot be produced in life without the rejection of false and perverted values and the adoption of pure and healthy ideals. This, precisely, is what *Lā Ilāha Illallāh* means. The first part of it consists of the denial of fictitious deities and absolute rejection of the materialism and the second of the implicit affirmation of faith in the Almighty, the Glorious One. The tragedy of the West is that it quickly fulfilled the first part of the Confession, challenged the overlordship of the Church in the Middle Ages and put and end to the tyranny of the Pope, but where the other part was concerned it was a total failure. Human society cannot thrive only on negative virtues. Europe, which had established superiority over the world through knowledge, discipline and force, failed in the real sphere of life. It was bankrupt from within, possessing neither a living faith, noble ideals nor healthy objectives. It went astray and became concerned with ignorance and error.

Iqbal's cheerful hopefulness does not permit him to lose faith in the future of the East. He is a firm believer in its revival and resuscitation. In the present poem he says that the East is full of latent power and promise of development and expresses the hope that from the "motionless sea" will rise a powerful tidal wave that will sink the boat of corruption and injustice. He protests against the designs of the Western Imperialists who have made the East the main target of their conspiracies and enslaved its mind and spirit. The Easterner has drifted away from his mental and spiritual beliefs and has become a person of no importance in the world. Slavery makes a man blind and distorts his judgement. Only the understanding and power of discrimination of free and self-respecting people is reliable.

> Modern Civilisation is filled to the brim with the wine of *No and No*,
> But the goblet of Affirmation the Saqi does not hold;
> The dextrous fiddler's chords have kept it subdued,
> In the lowest string murmurs the wail of Europe's woe;
> From the self-same flood which breeds the crocodile,
> Rises the savage wave that destroys its lurking place below.
> And what is slavery? Exile from the love of grace and beauty,
> Nothing is ever lovely but if freemen call it so,
> In the bondsman's sight we never put our trust,
> The sight of the freeborn alone is dependable in the world,
> The master of Today is he who by his own resolve,
> Has finished Tomorrow's pearl from the deep oceans of Time.

The West has popularised the cult of delicacy and refinement and has thus softened men's belief and faith. The deceitful craftsman has melted the rock. However, Iqbal claims that he has also overcome the arrogance of many an oppressor with the "luminous hand" of faith and contentment. Love teaches man to be self-respecting and makes him distrustful of worldliness and fortune hunting and this is what enables and inspires him to rise to the dizzy heights of ecstasy. He proclaims that no one should wonder if the planets become the true Believer's stepping-stones, for if he lives his life according to the message of God and follows the leadership and guidance of the blessed Prophet, then he will gain great knowledge and awareness that will in the future give out the light of the Valley of Sinai.

> The glassblowers of Firangistan[73] can make stone melt and flow,
> But glass bathed in my elixir becomes as hard as flint.
> Though Pharaohs plotted, and yet plot against me what harm?
> In my sleeve I possess the luminous hand of Moses.
> This spark how can it be subdued by earth's rubbish heaps,
> Hath not God create it to burn bare whole deserts?
> Love is self-beholding, Love the self-sustaining thing,
> Love stands Unconcerned at the gates of Caesar and Chosroes.
> What wonder if the Plaedias or the high moon fall my prey,
> For I have bound my head to the Prophet's saddlebow!
> The Path-finder, Last Messenger of God, Master of all,
> Who on the road-dust bestowed the splendour of Sinai?
> In the high-wrought eye of Love He is the first and the last,
> The Book, the Word, the Chapter and the Verse.
> Out of respect for Sinai I did not go pearl diving or else
> Countless gems still cluster in this deep, bottomless sea

CHAPTER FIFTEEN

PRAYER OF TARIQ

When the young and courageous Muslim General, Ṭāriq bin Ziyād, landed with his Arab soldiers on the coast of Spain he ordered the boats in which they had crossed the Mediterranean to be burnt so that there remained no possibility of a retreat. After the command had been carried out he addressed his troops in these memorable words; "There is now no escape. The sea is behind you and the enemy is in front. By God! You have nothing to depend upon except your own courage and fortitude." The soldiers became enthusiastic rousing speech and their trust in God and in the strength of their own arms became complete.

Ṭāriq realised that the Spaniards were far superior to them in numbers and equipment, and being cut-off from home by hundreds of miles he could also not hope for reinforcements. His only hope lay in capturing the arms of the enemy otherwise there would be no hope of triumph. Ṭāriq was worried, and, in the desperateness of his situation, he could think of no other resource than to seek Divine help by building up on the spiritual stamina of his men. He placed his reliance on the help of God and took it for granted that it was with him for he was sure of the justice of his cause. He knew in his heart that his army was the "party of Allah," which had not embarked upon the expedition for conquest or worldly glory but solely for the victory of his word and the defence and advocacy of his faith. They had come out with their "heads on their palms" to lead mankind from darkness to light and to deliver it from the overlordship of fellow men to the overlordship of Allah, the Supreme-Being. They aimed to lead it from the narrow confines of this world to the vastness of the Hereafter and from the tyranny and oppression of other religions to the fairness and justice of Islam. Had the Lord of Lords, the Creator of all things, not promised victory to His servants who took up arms in order to fulfil this mission? *And that Our host, they verily would be the victors* (QURAN, 37:173).

The Arab General, at that fateful hour, turned meekly to God and asked Him earnestly for help. He was following the example of the sacred Prophet ﷺ who had led the first Muslim army and, after marshalling his troops on the battlefield of Badr, withdrew to a quiet corner, placed his forehead on the ground and cried out for Divine help. "O God!" he had said. "If these men are killed today thou shalt not be worshipped in the world."

Thus, Ṭāriq, following in the steps of his leader and master, made a prayer which military commanders seldom make. They just never think of it. Iqbal has heightened the beauty of it by casting it into his poetic style. His *Ṭāriq ki Du'a* ("The Prayer of Ṭāriq") reads:

> O Lord! These bondsmen have set out in Thy path for *Jihād*. They are the seekers of Thy Good Pleasure. They are mysterious as well as the keepers of mystery. Their true state and position is only known to Thee. Thou hast taught them high-mindedness and, now, they will not settle for less than world-leadership and Divine rule. These proud men listen or yield to no one save Thee. Deserts and rivers carry out their biddings and mountains turn into heaps of dust out of fear and respect for them. Thou hast made them indifferent to the riches of the worlds by installing Thy love into their hearts. But for the love of *Jihād* and the joy of martyrdom the kingdom of the earth holds no attraction for them. This is the magic of love. It is the ruling passion that has brought them to this remote land. It is the last wish and the greatest desire of a Muslim. The world is hovering on the verge of ruin. Only the Arabs, by laying down

their lives, can save it from falling into the abyss of destruction. Everyone is thirsting for Arab blood and this sacred blood alone can remove the malady. Forests and gardens, tulips and roses are pining for it to colour their cheeks. We have come to this strange country to irrigate it with our life-blood so that the withered crop of humanity may flourish again and springtime may return after the agonising spell of autumn.

> The Ghazis, these mysterious bondsmen of Thine,
> To whom Thou hast granted zest for Divinity.
> Deserts and oceans fold up at their kick,
> And mountains shrink into mustard seeds.
> Indifferent to the riches of the world it makes,
> What a curious thing is the joy of love?
> Martyrdom is the desired end of the *Mu'min*,
> Not spoils of war, kingdom and rule!
> For long has tulip in the garden been waiting,
> It needs a robe dipped in Arab blood.

Iqbal goes on:

> O Lord! Thou hast conferred Thy unique favours on these desert-dwellers and herders of camels. Thou vouchsafed them a new knowledge, a new faith and a new way of life. Thou gave them the wealth of *Adhān*, which is the standing call of *Tawḥīd*, arousing men from the slumber of ignorance. By means of it the Arabs put an end to the death-like stupor that had descended upon the world and gave it the glad tidings of a new dayspring. Life had lost its warmth and movement and centuries had passed over it in that state. It regained its momentum, started again on its journey and attained the destination of faith and love. The crusaders do not regard death to be the end of life but the threshold of a new existence.

> O God! Grant them the dignity of faith and enmity for Thy own sake (as was revealed in the prayer of Noah: *"My Lord! Leave not one of the disbelievers in the land"* (QURAN, 71:26)), so that this army may become a relentless sword and a fearful thunderbolt for heathenism and corruption and produce fear for it in the heart of the enemy.

> Thou made the desert-dwellers absolutely unique,

In thought, in perception, in the morning *Adhān*;
What from centuries, life had been seeking,
It found the warmth in the hearts of these men;
Death is the opener of the heart's door,
It's not the journey's end in their sight.
Revive, once again, in the heart of the *Mu'min*,
The lightning that was in the prayer of Leave Not.[74]
Wake up ambition in the breasts, O Lord,
Transform the glance of the *Mu'min* into a sword.

The soldier's prayer was granted and the Arabs gained a magnificent victory. The Christian Spain became Islamic Andalusia and a strong Muslim Kingdom was established that lasted for eight hundred years. Its downfall came only when the spirit of Ṭāriq and his valiant companions had died out amongst the Muslims and the high purpose that had brought them there was forgotten. The extinction of religious fervour and free-living and internal strife not only led to the end of Muslim rule in Spain but also endangered the very existence of the followers of Islam in that country until not one of them was left. Such has been the way of God with those that are negligent and ungrateful since the beginning of time. *Thou wilt not find for Our method aught of power to change* (QURAN, 17:77).

CHAPTER SIXTEEN

TO THE SAQI

Iqbal's *Saqi Nama* ("To the Saqi") is universally regarded as one of his more important poems. It is remarkable for its depth of meaning from the literary and technical point of view and is a unique work of its kind in the whole range of Urdu literature. It is, perhaps, the first *Saqi Nama* in Urdu to use philosophy in poetry. Even in Persian, Zahuri's *Saqi Namas* are very limited in their scope. The excellence of Iqbal's art lies in his ability to transform verse into something of lasting beauty and the poetry becomes rich and lyrical in effect despite being simple in language. Iqbal continually sets new standards and traditions in verse making.

In Persian and Urdu the *Mathnawis*[75] of Nasim and Mir Hasan, and other poets are mostly of a descriptive nature. These poems are good so far as narration of events is concerned but in order to maintain their grace and energy the writers of these long verses had to intersperse them with the *Ghazals*. On the other hand, Iqbal has maintained the emotional fervour of *Qasida* and *Ghazal* in *Mathnawi*, as well and has saved it from becoming dull and monotonous. Throughout, the style is elevated and vigorous yet musical and clear yet suggestive.

In the opening part of the *Saqi Nama* Iqbal describes the coming of spring but he uses the subjective treatment of Nature as a background to his poetry. He says that the spring has come, its heralds have spread over hills and dales, and tulips and roses, briars and basils have established their sway; the springtime has breathed life and vitality even into rocks, and clouds of bliss have enveloped the earth. In this delightful environment birds have come out of their nests and brooks and rivers, gushing forth from the mountains, are moving forward majestically in the plains like life itself, turning and twisting, halting and advancing, jumping and crawling, overcoming obstacles and circumventing obstacles.

Iqbal uses the spiritual significance of nature to convey his philosophy of life in the allegory of a mountain stream. Just as the stream advances steadily spite of obstructions, continually changing direction but never losing liveliness and energy, so should man develop his personality by overcoming his difficulties and refusing to surrender.

> Spring's caravan has pitched its tents;
> The mountain's skirts into paradise have turned.
> Rose, lily, narcissus, daffodil; the poppy,
> The eternal martyr, in bloodstained shroud.
> Behind the veil of colour earth has hidden,
> Even in the veins of stone blood is flowing.
> Blue is the sky; the air intoxicating,
> No feathered biped will stay in its nest.
> And look that mountain-stream leaping,
> Rebounding, slipping, gushing, stumbling,
> Jumping, swaying, crawling, recovering,
> Winding its way in spite of curve and bend,
> Forces its way through the boulder when it stops,
> It pierces the hearts of mountain rocks.
> Oh Saqi! Vermillion checked-see!
> Life's message how the brook conveys.
> Pour me the fiery, veil-burning wine,
> Not every day the springtime comes,
> The wine by which life's soul is illumined,
> Which sustains the universe keeps it alive,
> Holds the strife and tumult of eternity,
> The wine by which eternal secret is revealed;
> Oh Saqi! Raise that mystery's curtain!
> Let the wagtail challenge falcon's wing!

To the Saqi

The times have changed and the hidden motives of the West have been exposed and its conspiracies against the East have been spelled out. The revolution that has taken place in the minds of men has unnerved the Western leaders. The sterility of Western politics and the absurdity of its outdated traditions have come to light and concepts like those of Imperialism and Colonialism are being openly challenged. The Capitalist age is nearing its end as the masses are beginning to show signs of wakefulness.

Though the Muslim knows he must believe in Monotheism, abandonment of his faith is still a problem for him and his learning, culture, philosophy and mysticism are not secure against the inroads of pantheistic doctrines. Reality is being eroded by superstition and the *Millet* has yet far to go to shake of the spell of fantasy and folklore. Preachers and orators give ideas from the pulpit but although academic they are lacking in sincerity and earnestness and thus fail to reach the hearts. The Sufi who was known for human sympathy, quest for truth and religious lofty-mindedness has got lost in mystic visions and trances, and, on the whole, Islam has come so close to decline that the Muslim's has lost the spark of faith and his life has become synonymous with death.

> The fashions of the Age have turned round,
> The tune is new; the orchestra has changed;
> The wiles of the Frank have been laid bare,
> The Frankish glass blower is bewildered, confused;
> Old statecraft is a cause of shame,
> Of king and sovereign the earth is sick,
> The day of Capitalism is done,
> The juggler has shown his tricks and gone.
> The Chinese, long sunk in stupor, are waking up,
> Himalayan streams, again, are gushing forth,
> The hearts of Sinai and Faran lie pierced,
> To fill his eyes with light, Moses is keen.
> But the Muslim, strident in the affirmation of *Tawḥīd*,
> Still wears the sacred thread in his heart,
> His art, law, logic and theology,

> Worshippers all of the idols of *'Ajam;*
> Truth in jargon has been lost,
> The Ummah caught in ritual maze,
> The preacher's phrase may delight the ear,
> But of love's fervour it is completely bare,
> Well set in logic his sermon is,
> And bedecked with the intricacies of idiom.
> The Sufi, God's servant once,
> Peerless in love, unmatched in honour,
> In the ideas of *'Ajam* has forgotten himself,
> This traveller has got lost in the Stages of the Soul.
> Love's fire is dead, darkness abounds,
> A Muslim? No; a heap of ashes is he!

Iqbal asks God to revive the spirit of faith among the Muslims and restore to them the glory of olden days. He begs Him to rekindle the flame of love so that they can attain to heights that are inaccessible to the materialists. He prays from the pulsation of the heart of 'Alī and the singleness of purpose of Abū Bakr to be granted once again to the Muslim *Millet* and also the "warmth of eagerness," which is the distinctive attribute of living nations:

> O Lord! Thy earth and Thy heavens are real and Thy Power is eternal. Share its secret with the Muslim youth also and produce in its heart the tumult of life. On the Muslim young men bestow some of my love, anxiety and insight, pull my boat out of the storm and guide it safely to the shore. Reveal to me the mystery of life and death. Thou, indeed, art the Knower, the Well-Informed. O God! Thou hast made my nature a mirror in which the spirit of the times is reflected and the image of Divine inspiration is drawn. In my heart the battle between good and evil, belief and disbelief, faith and scepticism is perpetually waging. These are my riches and I implore Thee to distribute this pitiful fortune, these beggar's chattels, to the youth of Islam which alone is the rightful heir to them.

> Pour again the vintage wine, O Saqi,
> Let the same cup rotate!
> Lend me love's wings to soar on,
> Like a glow-worm cause my dust to fly!

To the Saqi

Release intellect from slavery's bonds,
Make youth instructor to old age.
Your moisture keeps the *Millet's* bough,
From Thy breath it draws its life.
Endow our hearts with the power to throb,
With ʿAlī's passion and Ṣiddīq's warmth!
Pierce our souls with that same arrow!
In our breasts awaken desire!
Hail, stars of Thy heavens; and hail to those,
Who on earth devote their nights to prayer!
Bestow on the youth the warmth of my heart,
My love and my vision!
Through whirlpools bring safe my boat,
Stationary it has become, set it afloat.
Teach me the secret of death and life,
You in whose sight infinite regions are!
Wakefulness of my tearful eyes;
The anguish concealed in my heart,
The torment of my midnight wail,
Poignancy of my loneliness in company,
My longings and my desires,
My hopes and my quests;
My nature, the mirror which reflects the world,
The pasture where thoughts like gazelles wander;
My heart; life's battleground, in which
Armies of doubt set upon faith's steadfastness.
These the world-scorners wealth, by which
Oh Saqi! Even in poverty I am rich;
That wealth bestow on my caravan,
Bestow-for there its place belongs.

Iqbal then expounds his philosophy of existence and brings to attention the force, changeability and fundamental unity of life.

Each moment flows the ocean of life,
From all things is manifest the rush of life.
Peace and permanence a mere illusion,
Each atom throbs, pulsates with life.
Caravan of existence never makes a halt,
Every moment the glory of creation is renewed:

> Thinkest thou that life is a riddle?
> Nothing but the passion of flight it is!
> Means of sustenance to it is travel,
> Movement is truth, halting a delusion.

Lastly, the poet warns the Muslim youth not to give in to worldly temptations, as they will rob him of his pride. What makes wealth desirable is that it enables one to live with honour. However, Iqbal tries to tell the Muslim young men that it is more important to live with an honest character and a good reputation. He says to them that the mysteries of love's genuflexion, which makes a man indifferent to all other acts of devotion and prostration, free him. He instils into them the love of adventure and urges them on to forge ahead and discover new worlds that lie beyond the imagination of the scientists. Iqbal insists that the transitory world of matter, with all its charms and inducements, is only the first and, by no means, the last stage in the journey of self-knowledge. The restless soul of man has not been created for the earth. It is not man's real home or cherished goal. He can be master of the universe but the universe cannot be his origin. A Muslim is nothing if he is not fearless and he should always be moving forward in his journey and fighting against crude materialism. Iqbal wants him to overcome the barriers of time and space because when the *Mu'min* reaches the stage of complete self-realisation the earth and the heavens become his and he begins to rule over the universe. The material world is not the be-all and end-all of creation as there are many other worlds, unknown and undiscovered. The process of creation is a continuing one. It has not come to an end. "The world is waiting for you to take the lead," says he to the Muslims. "It is a continually growing world, bursting and burgeoning at every instant. It is a free, dynamic process, not a static existence. It expands itself in proportion to the frontiers of your thought and endeavour. The vicissitudes of time are meant to give you an opportunity to discover yourself. You are

To the Saqi

the conqueror; the subjugator of whatever there is between the heavens and the earth. The angels aspire from the heights which belong to you, but they cannot challenge comparison with you."

> What is that breath's tide but a sword?
> And what is Ego but that sword's keen edge?
> Ego is life's innermost secret,
> The wakefulness of the universe,
> Drunk with glory, enamoured of solitude,
> All an ocean mewed in a drop of water,
> Eternity before it, eternity behind,
> No frontiers stand before it, nor at its back.
> The bread that takes away Ego's lustre,
> For him who guards his Selfhood is poison,
> Honourable alone is the bread for him,
> Which keeps the head held high.
> Your flame is not from the earth, but the earth from you,
> Other worlds exist, unknown, unseen,
> The essence of existence is not yet void.
> The sum and end of Time's revolution,
> That you should come to know yourself.

CHAPTER SEVENTEEN

THE LAMENTATION OF ABU JAHL

In the world of fantasy, ʿAmr bin Hishām (popularly known as Abū Jahl[76]), one of the most audacious defenders of ignorance and most zealous spokesmen for Arab nationalism makes a pilgrimage to Makkah which has now become the centre of faith and Monotheism and the citadel of Apostleship. In the *Ḥaram* instead of the idols of Lāt and Manāt, he sees earnest devotees of the Lord performing the circumambulation, celebrating the service and keeping their nights alive with prayer and supplication. A picture of *Rukūʿ* (bowing) and *Sujūd* (bowing to the ground), *Tasbīḥ* (glorifying Allah), *Tahlīl* (repeating the testimony of Allah's oneness), *Taḥmīd* (praising Allah), and *Tamjīd* (declaring the majesty of Allah), *Dhikr* (remembering Allah) and *Istighfār* (seeking Allah's forgiveness) appears before him. There are neither the idols of materialism, nor the images of Ignorance. Instead of glorifying *Hubāl, ʿUzza, Usaf* and *Nāʾila*[77] the Muezzin[78] proclaims the oneness of God and the Apostleship of Prophet Muḥammad ﷺ. Human equality and Islamic fraternity have taken the place of Pagan pride and tribal vanity. People now regard mankind to be a single family in which the Arabs and the non-Arabs are equal. The only thing that is superior is piety and moral excellence.

Abū Jahl listens attentively to the conversation of the Arabs but nothing boastfully personal, tribal or racial is said. He moves among the people and is shocked to find that no one looks down upon the other because of his origin or occupation. Instead, men are flocking round a black slave to receive instruction from him and they are proud of being his pupils. Abū Jahl tries his best to discover a trace of Paganism and ignorance in their religious beliefs and moral and social behaviour but is sorely disappointed. Ultimately, he realises that the marks of the past life have been completely obliterated and a new society based upon ethical and spiritual values has come up. The patterns of conduct, the standards of virtue and the notions of right and wrong have changed and a revolution has taken place both in the inner and outer existence of the Arabs. Abū Jahl feels deeply hurt at the radical turn of events and in his despair recites the following verse.

> No more the people that I knew,
> No longer the houses I frequented!

The chief of the tribe of Makhzūm[79] has become a foreigner in his own country and a stranger in his own home. He cannot recognise his old Makkah of which he was once a respectable citizen. How tremendously has it altered! He remembers the House of Ka'ba, the Hatīm,[80] the Black Stone, the Well of Zam Zam and the assembly of the Quraysh leaders in where they used to torment the Muslims. Has he lost his way and come to some other place?

He remembers the olden days when he considered the new faith of Muḥammad ﷺ a threat to Arab nationalism and to the hegemony of the Quraysh and held the Islamic way of life to be a challenge to Pagan customs and practices.

Abū Jahl believed that the Arabs were far more honourable and superior than the other races who he saw as mean and barbaric. He had foreseen the revolutionary consequences of Islam and knew that if it came out triumphant it would be the end of everything that was important to him. He was thus in the forefront in the defence of Paganism.

As Abū Jahl is lost in his thoughts about Paganism. He hugs the walls of the Ka'ba and complains against the sacred Prophet:

The Lamentation of Abū Jahl

My heart is bleeding and my soul is wounded. Muḥammad has put out the lamp of the Kaʿba and brought its honour to dust. He has razed the palaces of Caesar and Chosroes, kings and emperors, to the ground and done away with the old order by declaring: *Lo! The earth belongs to Allah. He bequeaths it to whomever He wills among His servants!* (QURAN, 7:128). He has cast a spell over our younger generations so that they have turned against us and become the ardent admirers of his faith and personality. Can there be a greater blasphemy than *Lā Ilāha Illallāh* upon the recitation of which all the deities except One God mentioned in history become false and fictitious? He has erased the name of the ancient faith and flung to the winds the glory of Lāt and Manāt. How I wish the world took vengeance upon him! Isn't it strange that he rejects the visible deities but has sacrificed all that he had for the invisible one? He proclaims his faith in the manifest to be inferior to faith in the unseen. How can one believe in something that is not present or cannot be seen? Is it not the height of bigotry and self-delusion to prostrate oneself before the imperceptible? Can prostration before the unseen ever be as satisfying as before the solid images of stone?

My breast is riven and anguished by this Muḥammad,
His breath has put out the burning lamp of the Kaʿba;
He has sung of the destruction of Caesar and Chosroes,
He has stolen away from us our young men;
He is a magician, and magic is in his speech,
These two words *Lā Ilāh* are unbelief.
So he has rolled up the carpet of our father's faith,
And has done with our lord gods what he has done.
By his blow lie scattered Lāt and Manāt,
Take vengeance upon him, you wide world,
He bound his heart to the invisible, broke with the visible,
His incantation has destroyed the present image.
It is wrong to fix one's eye on the invisible,
That which not comes into sight, wherever is it?
It is blindness to make prostration to the invisible,
The new religion is blindness. Blindness is remoteness.
To kneel and bend low before an undimensioned God,

Such prayers bring no joy to the worshipper.

Abū Jahl laments that "the religion of Muḥammad has sounded the death-knell of nationalism. He belongs to the noble tribe of the Quraysh and yet shows respect to the slaves and treats the rich and the poor, the Arab and the non-Arab, alike. He even dines with his own slave. Alas! He did not realise the worth of the Arabs and made the Persian rustics and, black-skinned salves their equals. He has brought shame on the Arab race. I know that he has borrowed the concept of equality from Iran and fallen to the deception of Persians like Salmān. His imaginative mind has brought untold misery on the Arabs. The Hashimite young man has himself put an end to his nobility and his *Namaz* has made a simpleton of him. Can the pedigree of a Persian compare with ours? Can he ever talk in the Bedouin accent or cultivate the *Mudhiran*[81] manner of speech? O Arab intellectuals! Arise and destroy the myth of Muḥammad's inspiration. The Arab nationalism has got to come into its own."

> His faith cuts through the rulership and lineage of Quraysh,
> And denies the supremacy of the Arabs;
> In his eyes the high and low are the same,
> He ate out of the same dish with his slave.
> Ignorant of the worth of the noble Arabs,
> He fraternised with the uncouth Ethiopians,
> Redskins have been confounded with black skins,
> The honour of tribe and family has been destroyed.
> This equality and fraternity are of ʿ*Ajam*,
> I know well that Salmān is a Mazdakite,
> The son of ʿAbdullāh,[82] has been duped by him,
> And he has brought disaster upon the Arab people.
> Hāshim's progeny has become estranged one from another,
> The two *Rakʿāt* have utterly blinded them.
> What is ʿ*Ajam* stock, compared with the ʿAdnānī,[83]
> Can the dumb vie in eloquence with Sahbān?[84]
> The eyes of the elect of the Arabs have been darkened,
> Will you not rise up, Zubayr[85] from the dust of tomb,
> You who are for us a guide in this desert,

The Lamentation of Abū Jahl

Shatter the spell of the chant of Gabriel.

Turning to the Black Stone Abū Jahl asks why it does not support him. To Hubāl he says, "O Lord! Why don't you launch an attack on the faithless usurpers and drive them out of the ancient home? Advance with your companions or send a sandstorm to destroy them." "O Lāt and Manāt," Abū Jahl goes on mournfully, "Do not depart from our land, and, if you must, at least do not desert our hearts. Stay for a while, so that I may see you to my heart's content."

> Tell again, you Black Stone, now tell again,
> Tell again what we have suffered from Muḥammad,
> Hubāl, thou who acceptest the prayers of thy servants,
> Seize back thy home from the irreligious ones,
> Expose their flock to the wild wolves,
> Make their dates bitter on the palm tree,
> Let loose a burning wind on the air of the desert,
> As if they were stumps of fallen down palm trees.
> O Manāt, O Lāt, go not forth from this abode,
> Or if you must, go not from our hearts,
> You who have forever a lodging in our eyes,
> Tarry a little, if you intend to depart from me.

CHAPTER EIGHTEEN

ECHO OF PAGANISM

Having talked about every conceivable subject on the planet in *Javed Nama (The Song of Eternity)*, Iqbal then journeys to other planets and visits the Valley of Venus which he describes as the home of the ancient gods whom people used to worship during the days of Paganism and in whose name they carved images and built shrines and tabernacles. The influence of these deities was not restricted to belief and faith but had also permeated poetry and literature.

The idols of all the Pagan deities, of the Sun, Moon and Mercury, of the gods of Egypt and Yemen and the Lords of Iraq and Arabia and of the goddesses of union and separation were present in the valley. Their forms were different, due to the different sculptural skill of various peoples and communities; for example while one of them was holding a naked sword in its hand, the other wore a snake round its neck. However, whatever the differences in form and shape, their insides were identical. They were overwhelmed with the fear of the "Inspiration of Muḥammad" that had led mankind to revolt against their divinity and build up a new world on the basis of the Oneness of God.

When Mardukh carried the news of the poet's unexpected pilgrimage to Alha, he was overjoyed. Believing it to be fortunate for the god's and goddesses, Mardukh exclaimed, "Congratulations to you! Man again has turned his back upon Allah and is returning to us. Having rejected the divine faiths he is coming back to ancient mythology and folklore. It surely is a ray of hope that has appeared after a long, long time in our desolate place and a wind of good cheer that has risen from the enslaved earth."

> Mardukh said: "Man has fled from God,
> Fled from Church and Ḥaram, lamenting;
> And to augment his vision and perception,
> Turns his gaze backwards, to the past age.
> Time has turned a new leaf,
> A favourable wind is rising from yonder earth."

Baal, the god of the Phoenicians and the Canaanites, was the first to greet the poet who began to dance with joy:

> Man searched the skies but could not find a trace of God there either. It shows that the Divine Faith he boasts of is a myth. Religion is an idea that goes as quickly as it comes. It is like a wave, now rising; now subsiding. Man cannot attain self-fulfilment without a visible deity. Glory be to the Westerner who understood clearly the mentality of the East and revived us through the channels of study and research. Do not allow the golden opportunity to slip out of your hands, which the Western statesmen have made available. Even the descendants of Ibrāhīm have forgotten the creed of Monotheism and consigned the covenant of eternity to oblivion. They have lost the joy of believing and, in the company of the Franks, cast to the winds all that they possessed including the faith brought to them by archangel Gabriel.

> Man has rent asunder the azure roof,
> And, beyond the sky, seen no God.
> What is there in man's heart but thoughts,
> Like the waves, this rising and that subsiding?
> His soul finds peace in the manifest,
> Would that the past age might return!
> Long live the Frank, the knower of the East,
> Who has made us rise from the tomb!
>
> Behold, the ring of Unity is broken,
> Abraham's progeny has lost the joy of *Alast*,[86]
> Freeborn *Mu'min* has fallen into the bonds of directions,

> Joined up with fatherland and parted from God;
> His blood is frozen of the glory of the idolaters,
> The old man of the *Ḥaram* has tied the sacred thread.
> Ancient Gods, our time has come!

Hubal, in the same way, held forth: "The freeborn *Mu'min* who cared nothing for the distinctions of race, geography and nationality and knew not anyone save God, the Creator of the Worlds, he now not only loves the homeland but even worships it and fights for it while he does not devote a moment to Divine remembrance. Today the whole World of Islam is caught in a web of Western thought and even its religious leaders have become the imitators of the West. For us the time is most favourable to act. We ought to take delight in the defeat of the Islamic faith. Nationalism, ultimately, has triumphed and a thousand storms of Abū Lahab are raging to blow out the lamp of Muḥammad. It is true we still hear the sound of *Lā Ilāha Illallāh* but only from the lips. It does not spring from the hearts and what is not rooted in the heart does not remain for long also on the lips. The magic of the West has once again plunged the world into darkness and ejected religion. These disciples of ours are doing excellent work. They have renounced the world and taken refuge in caves and forests. We had released our followers from the duties of worship and obedience and allowed them complete freedom from restraint. We had given them singing and clapping in the place of solemn veneration and sanctified dancing and music. We did not believe in the dull and monotonous *Namaz* which was bereft of music. Our influence is still felt among men who like the visible idols better than the invisible God."

> The days of joy have returned to the world,
> Religion has been routed by country and lineage:
> What fear is there now from the lamp of Muṣṭafā,
> Seeing that a hundred Bu Lahabs blow it out?
> Though the sound of *Lā Ilāh* comes still!
> What leaves the heart how on the lips can remain?

Ahriman has revived the magic of the West,
The day of Yazdan[87] is pale with the fear of the night.

Band of religion from his neck must be loosed,
Our slave was ever a free bondmen;
Since the *Namaz* is heavy for him,
We seek only one *Rakʿah*, and that without prostration.
Passions are aroused by songs,
What pleasure is there in prayers without music?
Better than God who remains out of sight,
Is the demon that makes itself visible.
Ancient gods, our time has come!

CHAPTER NINETEEN

WITH JAMALUDDIN AFGHANI

During Iqbal's intellectual and spiritual journey, in the company of the sage Rūmī, he encounters some of the personalities of the past who had played a leading part in the history of Islam, particularly its later period. He is transported to a valley that has never known the conquest of man and which abounds in natural scenery, "a world of mountains and plains, seas and dry land." Iqbal wonders how such a place could remain free from the effects of civilisation.

Iqbal is deeply impressed by the idyllic surroundings and he hears the sounds of *Adhān* coming from a distance. Excited, he looks at Maulana Rūmī who tells him that they are in the valley of the Friends of Allah with which they have a close association. It was here that Adam had stayed for a few days after being commanded to leave Heaven and these expanses had felt his sighs and heard his lamentations at dawn. Only pious men, such as, Fuḍayl, Abū Saʿīd, Junayd and Bayazīd could dare make the pilgrimage to such a place. It is here that Maulana Rūmī invites Iqbal to offer the prayer of love, which they been denied in the material world.

They move on and see two men engaged in prayer, one of whom is Afghan (Jamāluddīn Afghānī[88]) and the other a Turk (Saʿid Halim Pasha[89]). Rūmī tells Iqbal that they are the noblest sons of the East. Both of them had relentlessly striven for emancipation of the East, particularly Jamāluddīn Afghānī. Saʿid Halim Pasba was a man of great vision and sincerity whose mind was as lucid as his soul was restless. Two *Rakʿāt* of *Namaz* offered behind them were more valuable than life-long devotions.

Jamāluddīn Afghānī recites *Sūrat al-Najm* (chapter 53 of the Quran) and a wave of excitement runs through the place. The appropriateness of the Sura coupled with the warm-heartedness of Jamāluddīn Afghānī and the beauty and sublimity of the Quran produce an atmosphere of rare feeling and intensity. So much so that Abraham and Gabriel would have been moved to ecstasy. The recitation of the vigorous leader could have made the cry of *No God but God* rise from the graves and bestowed ardour and ecstasy on David. Every mystery is revealed by the recital and the heavenly archetype stands unveiled.

After the *Namaz* is over, Iqbal humbly kisses the hand of the leader and Maulana Rūmī introduces the poet as a restless soul, a tireless traveller and an obdurate dreamer. He calls him *Zinda Rud* (The Living River). Afghānī asks him about the state of the world and of the Muslims. Iqbal replies:

> O my master! The Muslim community that had been raised up for the conquest of the world is caught in the tangle of religion and country. The strength of conviction has departed from it and it has begun to lose faith even in the universality of Islam. Consequently, it is leaning more and more on nationalism for support. The Turks and the Iranians are intoxicated with the West. They have walked into its trap. On the other hand, Communism is playing havoc with the honour and dignity of the *Millet*.

> The spirit is dead in the body through the weakness of faith,
> It despairs of the strength of the manifest religion;
> Turk, Persian, Arab intoxicated with Europe,
> And in the throat of each the fish hook of Europe;
> The East laid waste by the West's Imperialism,
> Communism has taken the lustre from religion and community.

Deeply hurt, as Jamāluddīn Afghānī is, by what the poet tells, he listens to him attentively. In the end, he remarks "The deceiver of the West has taught the lesson of Nationalism to the East. On his own part, he is always on the look out for new dominions, but wants to keep you permanently divided. You must, therefore, come out of its prison-house and play a universal role. The Muslim should regard every country his home. If you are prudent you will rise above the 'world of brick and stone.' Islam breaks the shackles of materialism and teaches self-awareness. He who realises God even the universe cannot contain him. Weeds come out of the dust and return to it, but with mankind it is different. His external existence is inclined towards the earth but inwardly he belongs to another world. The soul is ill at ease with material limitations. It is unaccustomed to restraints and restrictions. When it is shut in the cage of Nationalism it feels stifled. Falcons do not like to live in nests, what to speak of cages. The handful of dust we call country and to which we give the name Egypt, Syria or Iraq has, undoubtedly, a claim on us but it does not mean that we should confine ourselves to it and cease to look across its frontiers. The sun rises in the East but its rays fall on the East and West alike. It knows no bounds though its rising and setting is governed by the laws of time and space."

> What is religion? To rise up from the face of the dust,
> So that the soul may become aware of itself!
> He who has said God is He is not contained,
> Within the confines of the order of four dimensions,
> The body says, "Go into the dust of the roadway,"
> The soul says, "Look upon the expanse of the universe"!
> Man of reason, soul is not contained in life's limits,
> The free man is a stranger to every fetter and chain.
> Though it is in the East that the sun rises,
> Showing itself bold and bright, without a veil,
> Its nature is innocent of both East and West,
> Though by relationship, true, it is an Easterner.

Afghānī then says:

Communism is a figment of the Jew's imagination who mixed up truth with falsehood and whose mind was steeped in infidelity though his heart believed. It is a tragedy of the West that having lost sight of the transcendental truths it is trying to seek them out in matter and stomach. The vitality of the soul is not dependent on the body, but Communism does not go beyond the belly and womb. The creed of Karl Marx is founded upon the equality of stomachs while the roots of the brotherhood of man lie in love, fellow-feeling and compassion and not in physical equality.

> The Westerners have lost the track of the heavens,
> They go hunting for pure soul in the body.
> The pure soul takes not colour and scent from the body,
> And Communism has nothing to do save with the body.
> The religion of that apostle, who knew not truth,
> Is founded upon equality of the belly,
> The abode of fraternity being in the heart,
> Its roots are in the heart, not in water and clay.

With regards to Capitalism, Afghānī observes that, "However attractive it may seem its heart is dark, soul enervated and conscience dead. Like the honeybee it flits from flower to flower, sucking the nectar. The freshness of the flowers, apparently, suffers no loss but they actually die and little is left to choose between them and the paper-flowers. Likewise, Capitalism preys upon nations and individuals and reduces them to skeletons. Greed, godlessness and inhumanity are common to Communism and Capitalism. If life in Communism is *Khurūj* (production) in Capitalism it is *Khirāj* (taxation), and between these two stones the soul of man is caught like a glass. Communism is the enemy of humanity. Materialism is the article of faith with both of them. Their exterior is faultless and immaculate but the interior is guilty and reprehensible."

> The soul of both of them is impatient, restless,
> Both of them know not God, and deceive mankind.
> One lives by production, the other by taxation,
> And between the two stones man is caught like a glass.
> The one puts to flight science, religion, art,

> The other robs the body of soul, the hand of bread.
> I have seen them both drowned in water and clay,
> Both bodily bright, both utterly dark of heart.
> Life means a passionate burning, an urge to make,
> To cast in the dead clay the seed of a heart,

Afghānī complains that the Muslims behaviour does not conform to the teachings of the Quran. Confusion and discord have set in among them and their attachment to the Prophet ﷺ is a thing of the past. Today, the Muslims do not mould their individual and collective existence according to Quranic guidance and have become materially and spiritually backward. They have destroyed the despotic order of Caesar and Chosroes, but have themselves become the upholders of monarchy and patrons of un-Islamic states.

> In his heart there is no burning fire,
> Muṣṭafā no longer lives in his breast,
> The *Mu'min* has not eaten the fruit of the Quran,
> In his cup I saw neither wine nor dregs,
> He broke the magic spell of Caesar and Chosroes,
> And himself sat on the imperial throne.

To the Russians Afghānī sends the message that since, like the Muslims, they too have destroyed the order of Caesar and Chosroes, they should learn from their example and remain determined in the battle of life. After breaking the idols of monarchy and nationalism they should not even think of them for the world today needs a community that is stern as well as mild and severe as well as benevolent. The Russians should assimilate the religious and spiritual guidance of the East, as the West has grown inwardly bankrupt. Now that they have completed the stage of "negation" they must march onward in order for the goal of living affirmation to be reached. If they are really keen to establish a world order they should first provide themselves with a solid foundation which faith alone can furnish. Having rid the world order of superstition and materialism they should study the Quran verse by verse. They will then realise how the Quran is opposed to imperial rule and exploitation. It sentences Capitalism to death and assists the slave, the worker and the poor. It frowns upon the spending of wealth that may be in excess of one's needs and says that it would be better directed towards the poor. It prohibits money lending and sanctions commerce and advises people strongly to carry out deeds of monetary good like *Qarz-i-Hasna*[90] and *Sadqa-i-Jariya*.[91] The lending and repaying of money is the root of all evil in the world.

The Quran says that the land belongs to God. Man can put it to his use, but he is not the real owner. His position is that of a trustee. *And spend of that whereof He hath made you trustees* (QURAN, 57:7). Kings and sovereigns have used mankind selfishly. The Quran calls for truth and justice and declares the earth to be for the whole of the human race who make up a single family. *Your creation and your raising are only as [the creation and raising of] a single soul* (QURAN, 31:28). Hence, when the Quranic kingdom was established the extremist monks and hermits went into hiding and the magic spell of the Church was broken.

The Quran is much more than a book, for it reconstructs mankind. It creates a new man and, through him, a New World. It is the living gospel of guidance and happiness at the heart of the universe and humanity. The destinies of the East and of the West are bound up with it. A new law has been laid down and a new constitution has been enforced in the world. However, it is now essential to look at the world from the viewpoint of the Quran so that the reality of things is revealed to all.

> Who gave the "luminous hand" to the black man?
> Who gave the good news of no Caesar, no Chosroes?
> Without the Quran the lion is a wolf,
> The *Faqr* of the Quran is the root of kingship.
> The *Faqr* of the Quran is the mingling of meditation and reason,
> Without meditation I never saw reason mature.

With Jamāluddīn Afghānī

What is the Quran? Sentence of death for the master,
Succour for the slave without food and wherewithal.
It is lawful to draw one's sustenance from the earth.
This is man's wherewithal, the property of God.
When the Quran's design descended into the world,
It shattered the images of priest and pope.
I speak openly what is hidden in my heart.
This is not a book; it is something other!
When it has entered the soul; the soul becomes different,
When the soul has been changed, the world is changed,
Like God, it is, at one, hidden and manifest,
Living and enduring and, of course, speaking.
In it are destinies of East and West,
Produces the swiftness of thought like lightning.
It told the Muslim, "Put your life in your hands;
Give whatever you posses beyond your needs."
You have created a new law and constitution,
Look around a little in the light of the Quran,
Life's heights and depths you will come to know,
And you will understand the destiny of existence.

CHAPTER TWENTY

AT THE DOORSTEP OF THE PROPHET ﷺ

Love for the Prophet and yearning for Madinah were most important in Iqbal's life, and his poems are full of references to them. During the last phase of his life this tender yet all encompassing devotion had become so intense that he was moved to tears at the very mention of the name of Madinah. He was unable to make the pilgrimage to the blessed city due to his illness, but spiritually he was there all the time.

Iqbal speaks of the Holy Prophet in a thousand ways in his verses. Over and over again, he pays the tribute of love to him and while doing so draws a poignant picture of the Muslim *Millet*. On such occasions his poetic genius becomes the most developed it has ever been and is full of thought and emotion. The truths he had discreetly held back begin to unfold themselves freely and without constraint.

> In a word could the world of desire be told, but
> To stay in his presence I prolonged the story.

Some of Iqbal's most stirring poems have been written on the theme of love for the Prophet and they display a rare beauty both technically and creatively. In every line the poet makes us feel that he has something to say which is not only worth saying, but is also aimed at giving us pleasure.

In the verses we are going to reproduce the poet undertakes an imaginary journey to Arabia, to the twin cities of Makkah and Madinah. In eager expectation he presses on. The sand under his feet appears to be softer than silk and every particle of it seems to have turned into a beating, throbbing and pulsating heart. He tells the camel driver to watch out for those tiny hearts and move slowly.

> Blessed be the desert whose evenings cheerful as the dawn,
> Whose nights are short and days exalted;
> Tread softly, O traveller! Softly still,
> Each particle here is afflicted like us.

The song of the *Hadi-Khwan*[92] intensifies his restlessness, the wounds of his heart re-open and verses of breathtaking elegance begin to take shape spontaneously.

Still elevated, Iqbal visits the *Muwājaha*[93] of the Holy Prophet and sends respectful *Durood* (benediction) and *Salām* (salutation) to him. Love takes over his whole being and taking advantage of the precious moments the poet unburdens himself of his feelings and relieves his mind by speaking of the woes and worries of the Muslims. He complains of the utter helplessness of the Islamic world, its shameful capitulation to the Western Civilisation and the utter disregard of his message by his own people.

Iqbal has called this collection of verses *Armughan-i-Hejaz* ("The Gift of Arabia") and it is a most valuable offering for the entire Islamic world.

> Musk-laden is the zephyr today,
> Beloved's tresses, haply, are loosened in wind's direction.

Iqbal made this spiritual journey when he was more than sixty years old and in ill health. At that age people usually retire from active life. However, the poet still embarked upon the arduous undertaking because it was in response to the call of love and in fulfilment of the high aim of his life.

> Despite old age I took the way to Yathrib,[94]
> Singing with the ecstasy of love,
> Like the bird which in the evening,
> Spreads its wings eagerly for the nest.

He wonders why is going to Madinah, which was the true dwelling-place of the soul and the real home of the *Mu'min*, at such a late period in his life would be seen as strange. Just as the birds at sunset fly back to their nests, his spirit, too, was restless to return to the place to which it actually belonged.

As Iqbal's camel gathers speed he tells it to go slow as the rider is weak and infirm but it pays no heed and continues to trot joyously as if a silk carpet had been spread for it.

> At morn I told the camel to take it easy,
> For the rider is old and sick,
> But it goes on merrily as if,
> The sand under its hooves is silk.

The caravan presses on with its offerings of *Durood* and *Salām* and, in that entrancing atmosphere Iqbal wishes to perform the genuflexion of love on the burning sands that would leave a permanent mark on his forehead and advises his companions to do the same.

> Blessed is the desert in which the caravans,
> Recite the *Durood* as they press forward,
> Carry out on its hot sands the prostration,
> That burns the forehead and leaves its mark.

Iqbal begins to sing verses from *Iraqi* and *Jami*[95] and this makes the people wonder in what language the lines were as they filled their hearts with agony and made them forget hunger and thirst even though they did not understand their meaning.

> Tell, caravan-leader, who the non-Arab is?
> His song is not of Arabia;
> But the tune is refreshing to the heart,
> So that one could live in the desert without water.

Iqbal takes pleasure in the hardships of the journey, and exhaustion and loss of sleep comfort him. The journey is not long and tiring for him and he has no desire to reach his destination quickly. On the contrary, he begs the camel-driver to take an even longer route so that the period of waiting is extended.

> Let the traveller's suffering be more delightful,
> And his lamentation even more frenzied;
> Take a longer route thou camel-driver,
> And make the fire of separation burn stronger.

The poet thus completes the journey and arrives at Madinah. He says to his travelling companion, "We both are the prisoners of the same ringlet. The opportunity has, at last, come to us to fulfil our heart's desire and spread our eyelashes at the feet of the beloved. Let us lift restrictions from our eyes and allow the storm that is brewing in them to have a full play."

> Come, O friend, let us weep together,
> We both are victims of beauty's aureole;
> Give a free rein to what lies buried in the heart,
> And rub our eyes at Master's feet.

Iqbal marvels at his fate and is proud of the fact that a worthless beggar like him has been favoured with presence in the magnificent durbar to which kings and savants fail to gain admission.

> The worth of the wise men was rated low,
> And to simpleton a rapturous glimpse was granted,
> How blessed, indeed, and how fortunate,
> The sovereign's door for the beggar was opened.

Even in that hour of supreme bliss Iqbal does not forget the Muslims, especially those of India and describes their pitiful state eloquently.

> The Muslim, that beggar with the air of kings,
> Some of the sigh from his bosom has fled,
> He weeps, but why? He does not know,
> A glance at him, O Apostle of Allah.

He feels that the tragedy with the Muslims is that they have fallen from a great height and the higher the place from which one falls, the more one is hurt.

> Of the afflicted beggar what to tell,
> The Muslim of noble descent;
> God bless the brave, hardy man,

From a high terrace he has fallen!

The Muslims are disunited and leaderless and this is the main cause of their misery. They are a collection of individuals with no unanimity of action or attitude.

> The blue sky is still unkind,
> Aimlessly the caravan wends its way,
> Of their disunity what to speak,
> You know the Muslims are without a leader.

The Muslims have ceased to create men of outstanding stature, which was once their speciality.

> His blood that heat possesses no more,
> In his garden the tulips have ceased to grow,
> His scabbard as empty as his purse,
> The Book lay on the shelf in his desolate home.

Iqbal grieves at the change that has come over the Muslims. The joy of seeking has deserted their hearts and they have become lazy and ease loving. They have become accustomed to the crude pleasures of life and thus the call of the men of freedom makes no impression on them.

> His heart he made a captive of hue and scent,
> And emptied it of desire and yearning;
> The loud cry of the falcon they seldom hear,
> Whose ears get used to mosquito's humming sound.

In the eyes of the Muslim there is neither the light of faith nor the intoxication of love. His heart does not beat any longer for "someone," and pays no attention to "anyone's" remembrance. He is far removed from the state of "nearness" and very much away from the "desired goal."

> In his eye neither light nor joy,
> Nor the heart in his bosom restless;
> God help the *Millet* whose death,
> Is from soul devoid of presence.

Iqbal compares the present conditions of the Muslims with their glorious past and complains reverentially to God that those whom He had brought up with true faith and belief are now seeking the pleasures of life in other lands.

> Ask me not his condition,
> The earth is as mean to him as the sky;
> The bird Thou hast brought up on fruit,
> For it the quest of grain in the desert is unbearable.

The poet then speaks of the atheism that is becoming problematic in the Islamic world. As a scholar of philosophy and economics he knows that godlessness is making its way into the Muslim World through materialism, spiritual emptiness and cold heartedness. Furthermore, the extravagant ways of living are adding fuel to the fire. Iqbal believes that only love, righteousness and the pattern of life that Abū Bakr al-Ṣiddīq has set can challenge atheism. The whole world will then be obliged to treat them with respect.

> Irreligiousness has shaken the world,
> From the attributes of body they deduce about soul;
> Out of the *Faqr* Thou bestowed on Ṣiddīq,
> Produce restlessness for this lover of ease.

The real cause of the degradation of the Muslims is not poverty but the loss of the love that they once used to carry in their hearts. When these beggars used to bow before nobody except God, they became like kings, but as the inner fire died out in them they took refuge in shrines and monasteries.

> The beggars till they mustered in the mosque,
> They tore the collar of the kings;
> But when the fire within them died,
> The Muslims sought shelter in the shrines.

Iqbal looks carefully into the record of the Muslims and discovers enough in it to fill him with shame. Their conduct has nothing to do with the teachings of the Prophet and the precepts of Islam. Sorrowfully, he admits that the limits of debasement such as the worship of non-God and insincere praise of tyrannical rulers mean that the Muslims are clearly unworthy of God and have no right to be associated with Him.

> No one but ourselves I have to blame,
> We proved not worthy of Thy Grace.

The Islamic world has grown sterile and bankrupt. The ewers of Sufi-lodges are empty, the seminaries have become hollow and imitative and poetry and literature show no signs of life.

> Ewers of Sufi-lodges contain no wine,
> From the assembly of poets I rose dejected,
> Melody from the reed comes out dead.

The poet says that he went around the Islamic World but he the fearless, undaunted Muslim of whom death itself was afraid was unable to be found.

> I flew with the wings you gave me,
> And burnt myself with the fire of my song;
> The Muslim that made death tremble with fear,
> I searched in the world but did not find.

Analysing the cause of the frustration and waywardness of the Muslims, Iqbal remarks that if an individual or community possesses the heart but does not have the loved one it is bound to be devoid of peace as its energies are wasted and its endeavours lack cohesion.

> One night before God I wailed,
> Down in the world why Muslims are?
> Came the reply: "Don't you know,
> This community possesses the heart but not the beloved?"

Despite these dreary circumstances, Iqbal is not disheartened. He has neither lost hope in the Muslims nor despaired of the mercy of God. On the other hand, he is severely critical of the prophets of doom and of those who rely thoughtlessly upon others and look at everything through their eyes. Saddened, he observes that the custodians of the *Ḥaram* have become the keepers of the idol-temple, their faith has lost its vitality and their vision is not their own.

> Custodian of the Ḥaram is idol-hall's architect,
> His faith is dead and eyes not his own;
> From his look it is plain,
> He has lost all hope in the possibility of good.

Though the Muslims are weak and helpless they possess more moral principles than the kings. If their due place is given to them then their charm will turn into all-conquering strength.

> Though the Muslim is without corps and battalions,
> His soul is the soul of a king;
> If he gets his rightful place again,
> His charm is overwhelming.

Grieving over the injustice and insensitivity of the times Iqbal says:

> Occasionally I go and occasionally rise,
> What blood do I shed without a sword!
> Cast a loving glance from the terrace,
> I am up in arms against my Age.

Iqbal's whole life was spent struggling against the modern world. He exposed the crude materialism of the Western Civilisation, rejected it and guided the growing generations. He was a rebel as well as a reformer and a revolutionary as well as a redeemer.

> Like Rūmī I gave my *Adhān* in the Ḥaram,
> From him I learnt mysteries of the Self,
> He, during the mischief of their bygone days was born,
> And I, during the mischief of the present times.

The poet speaks proudly of his revolt against the modern educational system and tells how he managed to preserve his faith and individuality in the midst of trials and temptations. Faced with Western thought he claims to have displayed the supreme indifference of Hazrat Ibrāhīm (Abraham).

> The spell of modern education I broke,
> I picked the grain and left the net alone,
> God knows how in the manner of Ibrāhīm,

At the Doorstep of the Prophet

I sat in its fire easy in mind.

Iqbal regards his stay in Europe to have been, on the whole, barren and unproductive. Dry books, vain philosophical disputations, alluring beauty and pleasing sights were all that there was to remember. If he gained anything from it was self-abandonment that nearly deprived him of Selfhood.

> I gave my heart to Frankish idols,
> In the heat of temple-dwellers I melted;
> Such a stranger I became in my own eyes,
> That when I saw myself I could not recognise.

Even now when he recalls the dull and dreary time he spent in the West he feels sad and frustrated. He complains that Europe gave him nothing but a headache and he had an altogether depressing experience in the company of Western intellectuals.

> I imbibed wine in the alehouse of the West,
> And with my life I purchased headache;
> I sat in the company of wise men of Europe,
> And never had spent a more unprofitable time.

Iqbal then, humbly addresses these words to the Prophet: "I have been brought up on thy loving glance. The fine arguments and weighty discussions of men of learning make me sick. I am a petitioner at your door, a beggar of your street. Why should I dash my head against the doorstep of anyone else?"

> I am a beggar and from you I ask what I do,
> In my wretched body I want a mountain-hewing heart;
> Philosophical discourses give me pain in the head,
> For I have been brought up on your loving glance.

The poet turns his attention to Muslim theological doctors, the Ulema, who are supposed to be the custodians of religious knowledge and he expresses his disgust at their intellectual sterility. Their Arabian Desert possesses neither the spring of Zam Zam nor the House of Ka'ba even though the real worth of the desert of Arabia lies in these two landmarks of Allah.

> The heart of *Mulla*[96] is innocent of grief,

> His eye is seeing, but not moist,
> I rose from the seminary because,
> In his Arabian Desert no Zam Zam gushes.

Iqbal confesses that once he relied upon the non-God and was punished by being flung down from his place two hundred times. In this state, neither strength nor resourcefulness of mind prevail. It is the Divine will that prevails and even a minor aberration can be one's undoing.

> I placed my heart in nobody's hand,
> Myself the knots I unravelled,
> Upon other than God I once relied,
> And fell down from my station two hundred times.

For Iqbal, the modern age is heartless and hypocritical and in it man has become a cog in the wheel. What can Iqbal do other than brood over the gloomy turn of events?

> My eye is indifferent to what I see,
> The heart is melting in inner fire;
> Me, and the soulless, unfeeling times,
> What an enigma it really is? Tell me!

A feeling of loneliness oppresses Iqbal. In the wide world he is without a friend and sympathiser. He is his own consoler and comforter.

> In the East and the West I am a stranger,
> Friendless and forlorn, no confidant have I:
> I relate my sorrow to my own heart,
> How innocently loneliness do I cheat.

No one listens to him nor wants to learn from him and his fall on deaf ears. The Muslims see him as merely a poet and not a Believer who is revealing reality.

> They understand not the secret I reveal,
> Nor eat the fruit of my tree:
> O leader of nations! I seek justice from you,
> They look upon me as a reciter of *Ghazal*.

The command of the Holy Prophet is that he should carry

the message of life and eternity to mankind but the world only wants him to compose ordinary rhymes.

> You command me to sing of eternity,
> And impart to dead the message of life:
> But these unknowing men demand,
> That I record in verses the dates of the death of this man and that.

Iqbal complains of the indifference of his people to the knowledge and message that is the essence of his poetry. He wanted to make the offering of his heart but no one was willing to accept it.

> I've placed my heart on the palm but there were no takers,
> I possess the merchandise but where's the plunderer?
> Come and make my bosom your home,
> Because no Muslim is lonelier than me.

In the end, Iqbal speaks to Ibn-i-Saud of Arabia but what he tells him is really meant for all the rulers of the Muslim world. He warns King Saud against placing reliance on the foreigners and advises him not to trust anyone except God and himself. "If the rope is yours," says he, "you can pitch the tent wherever you like. But you will have no freedom of movement if it is a borrowed one. Try to know yourself. You occupy such a privileged position on the earth that your evening is more lustrous than the morning of others."

> Your station in the arid desert is such,
> That like the moon your evening shines as mirror;
> Pitch your tent wherever you want,
> To borrow rope from others is forbidden.

CHAPTER TWENTY-ONE

COMPLAINT AND PRAYER

Iqbal was a true Believer. His faith in Islam was without limit and for him Islam was the source of strength and the paramount mark of distinction in the world. Great knowledge was of no value before a simple, unsophisticated faith. In one of his verses he says that the ascetic possesses nothing other than an undying faith in *Lā Ilāha Illallah* and whilst the preachers and legal specialists have accumulated a pile of explanations and commentaries they have no idea of its fundamental significance. These *Korahs*, as he prefers to call them, have the wealth but not the heart to make use of it.

> The Dervish[97] possessed nought but the two words of *Lā Ilāh*,
> The legist of town is the Qarun of Arabic lexicon.

Devotion to the Prophet and loyalty to his message were more precious to Iqbal than life. In his opinion, to turn to any other source for instruction and enlightenment was derogatory to the spirit of love and self-respect.

> O master, keep an eye on the honour of your beggar,
> Who refuses to fill his cup from anyone else's stream.

Iqbal had been constantly ill since 1934 and went to stay at Bhopal for medical treatment. Despite his weak physical strength, his intellect remained as keen as ever and the state of Muslims never ceased to trouble him. He was still moved by the moral and spiritual degeneration of the Muslims, the scarcity of truly Islamic personalities among them and the infatuation of the growing generations for the Western Civilisation and their indifference towards their own values and ideals. Thus, he wrote an inspiring poem on April 13, 1936 in which he made a fervent appeal to the sacred Prophet and complained to him about the mental and material backwardness of the *Millet* and its debasement after elevation.

He said, "I beg to make an accusation against the *Ummah* which is, today, seized with the fear of death. You broke the idols of Lāt and Manāt, re-built the world and gave it a fresh lease of life. By virtue of it, belief and faith, ardour and earnestness and worship and piety command respect in the world and humanity is deriving joy and effulgence, and awareness and enlightenment from the Formula of Confession you taught. I, too, was born in an idolatrous land but rose above the worship of stones and animals. I neither submitted to monks and priests nor bent my knee before gods and goddesses nor kissed the doorsteps of kings and noblemen. It all is the gift of your faith and the fruit of your endeavours. I, also, have picked crumbs from your table-spread at which the whole world has been sitting and helping itself freely. Your personality and your sayings have been the focus of love and source of inspiration to the *Ummah* for hundreds of years. It is solely due to your teachings that it has remained self-respecting in poverty and lofty minded in indigence. However, today, the Islamic world has devaluated itself. It has lost a good deal of its worth and importance."

> Oh you, solace for us, the downtrodden,
> Deliver the community from fear of death.
> You destroyed Lāt and Manāt of old,
> And revived the timeworn world.
> Meditation and remembrance of man and *jinn*,
> You are the Morning Prayer, call of *Adhān*.
> Burning and ecstasy if from *Lā Ilāh*,
> In the night of doubt light is from *Lā Ilāh*.
> We made not God from quadruped,
> Nor bowed low before the hermit,

Nor bent the knee before the ancient gods,
Nor circumambulated round palaces of kings.
This, too, amongst your countless favours,
Our thought is the product of your teachings.
You remembrance the wealth of joy and ardour,
Which keeps the *Millet* proud in poverty.
Goal and destination of every wayfarer,
Your desire in the heart of each traveller.
Our harp, alas, has become so mute,
Plectrum is a burden upon its strings.

The poet goes on:

I travelled extensively in the Muslim World and visited the Arab and non-Arab countries but found that your followers were few and the disciples of Abū Lahab numerous. The mind of the Muslim youth is luminous but his heart is dark. He has become lazy and listless. Generations of Muslims have come up, one after the other, that are so thoroughly slavish in outlook that they cannot even dream of freedom. Modern education has deprived the Muslim young men of their spiritual heritage and rendered them ineffective. Unappreciative of their own worth, they are following the West blindly. They solicit arms from Western Powers and feel no hesitation in bartering away their souls. The eaglets have turned into wagtails, timid and fainthearted.

The mentors of the rising generations, good for nothing themselves, have failed to impart to them the lesson of Selfhood. They do not teach them what they really are and how can they discover themselves? In the fire of the West they are melting like wax.

The Muslim has forgotten the joy of martyrdom and lost faith in the Omnipotence of God. No one is all-powerful save Allah. He is concerned only with the transient life of the world and stretching a begging hand for a loaf of bread has become his profession. Instead of breaking the idols, the progeny of Ibrāhīm is carving and importing them from the West.

The present generation of the Muslims needs a renaissance. The command of *Rise by the Command of Allah* has to be given to it again. The West has not bewitched, but killed us without firing a shot. You upturned the thrones of Caesar and Chosroes, today, a man of faith is needed once more to break the spell of Western Civilisation.

> I wandered in ʿAjam and in Arabia,
> Bu Lahab in plenty, Muṣṭafā scarce.
> The Muslim youth, radiant of mind,
> His soul in darkness, without a lamp.
> Soft and delicate, silk-like, in prime,
> Desire from his bosom has departed.
> The slave, son of a slave, son of a slave,
> Liberty to his mind is strictly tabooed.
> Seminary has robbed him of the spirit of faith,
> Of it he knows only that it was.
> Stranger to himself, intoxicated with West,
> Seeker of barley-bread from the hand of the West.
> He bought a loaf in return for soul,
> And, in utter pain, made me groan.
> Picker of grain like a lowly bird,
> Knows not what the blue skies are!
> The schoolmaster, lacking in vision, narrow of mind,
> Never did he show him his place in the world.
> In the fire of the frank he has melted away,
> Hell it is, though of another make.
> *Mu'min* and yet ignorant of the mystery of death,
> *Lā Ghālib illallāh*[98] abides in his heart no more.
> Bewitched we are by the Civilisation of the West,
> Victims of the Frank without war and struggle.
> From among the people whose cup is broken,
> Raise up a God-intoxicated man of faith;
> So that the Muslim may rediscover himself,
> And rise above the world of time and space.

Iqbal cries to the Prophet:

> O glorious horseman of Arabia! For God's sake give me an opportunity to kiss your stirrup so that I may relate my agony, though my tongue is tied and a struggle is going on within me between love and deference. Love says, "Speak up; the friend is near," while respectfulness forbids. "Shut your mouth and

open the eyes," it tells. But eagerness is getting the better of restraint.

O horseman, pull the reins for a while,
Speech is not coming easy to me.
My feelings I may be able to express or not,
Love can at no time be subservient to respect.
One says, "Speak up, O afflicted one,"
The other: "Open your eyes and seal the lips."

O master! The poet says, "I am the rotten prey no hunter has cared to look at. I have run up to you. My voice is choking in my throat with emotion. The flame of the heart does not leap up to the tongue. The blazing breath of mine is charged no longer with inner heat. I am losing interest in the pre-dawn recitation of the Quran. The breath for which there is no place in the bosom can reside in it only as a prisoner. What it craves for are the boundless spaces of the firmament. Only in your glances lies the cure of my physical and spiritual ailments. Physicians' prescriptions do not agree with my withered soul. I cannot tolerate their bitter potions. Have pity on me and prescribe some palatable remedy. Like Busieri I beseech you to give me back the departed song. The sinners are more deserving of your intercession. Don't mothers show greater affection to their weakly children?"

Round you the universe rotates,
From you I beg a kindly glance.
My knowledge, thought, meditation are you,
My boat, ocean and storm are you.
The shrine of your street is my refuge,
Hopefully have I run up to you.
Ah! The agony of my body and soul,
A glance of yours is the sovereign remedy.
Like Busieri I beg deliverance from you,
That the day that was may return again.
Your mercy on the sinners is greater,
In forgiveness it is like the mother's love.

Iqbal continues: "I have always been at war with the worshippers of the night. Let my torch burn brighter. The period of your existence was the springtime of mankind, the season of flowers for the world. Why should a gust of the life-giving zephyr not come towards me and a ray of the world-illumining sun not light up a lowly particle of dust? The worth of the body is from the spirit and the spirit is from the breath of the beloved.

My intellect took me to the realms of philosophy and jurisprudence and enabled me to unravel the mysteries of Faith and *Sharīʿah*, but in the field of action my courage failed. My task is even harder than that of the Farhad. I need greater firmness and perseverance than him to put my capabilities to proper use in the contemporary world. I beg you to sharpen the edge of my sword. It is blunt, but the steel is well tempered.

Though I have wasted my life and ill-spent my youth, there is a thing called heart, which I have carefully preserved. I have always been proud of it for it has borne, from the first day, the imprint of your foot. The slave who is concerned only with the good pleasure of his master pays no attention to the world. For him separation from the master is death.

O Chosen One who endowed the Kurd[99] with the burning passion of the Arab! Listen to an Indian who has come to you with a bleeding heart. Even friends are not aware of his predicament. He is the flute that has got separated from its origin but in whose bosom sorrowful tunes are still rising in memory of the days of union.

I am the dry wood of the desert after setting fire to which the caravan moved away but which is still smouldering and waiting anxiously for another caravan to arrive and turn it into a blaze."

> O you whose existence world's early spring,
> Keep not your shadow away from me!
> The worth of body is from soul, you know,
> And the worth of soul is from the beloved.
> That I rely upon no one save God,
> Turn me either into a sword or key.
> Keen in the understanding of religion my intellect,

Complaint and Prayer

But seed of action in my field did not sprout.
Sharpen my axe for the task before me,
Is harder than even that of Farhad.
A believer, yes; no infidel am I,
Put me on whetstone, not of bad origin am I.
Though a barren tract my life has been,
I possess the thing they call the heart.
From the world's view I have kept it concealed,
Since it bears the imprint of your horse's hoof.
Your slave begs not solace from anyone else,
Life spent away from master is veritable death.
O you who endured the Kurd with Arab's burning,
Summon your own slave to your gracious presence.
Your slave is like a tulip with a scarred heart,
His grief even the friends do not know.
In the world like a flute he wails and wails,
Melody stabs his heart in quick succession.
Like half-burnt firewood in the arid desert,
The caravan has gone and I am smouldering still;
Waiting patiently in the wide, wild world,
That another caravan may pass along.
With the pang of separation my soul groans,
Fie upon me! Oh, fie upon me!

CHAPTER TWENTY-TWO

HISTORICAL TRUTHS AND ALLUSIONS IN IQBAL'S POETRY

Iqbal had never been a serious student of history and had never claimed to possess a thorough understanding of it. On the contrary, if he was asked to comment on a book written on a historical topic, he would plainly express his inability and say that history had never been a special subject of his study. Primarily, he was a scholar of Philosophy and, then, of the Quran. However, as is commonly known, Iqbal was a man of wide scholarship and deep erudition. He had carefully analysed the records of nations, communities, states and empires as well as religions, morals, cultures and civilisations. Thus, though history was not his subject, he was keenly concerned with the destiny of man and his problems, and with the rise and fall of nations and took an intelligent interest in the annals of his race. Moreover, thanks to the urge and ability to seek out truth and bring about harmony and co-ordination, he did not rest at the outer surface of events, but penetrated deep into the root of things. In this way, Iqbal succeeded in unfolding truths and drawing conclusions to an extent that was beyond the capacity of the majority of historians who lacked a philosophical background.

Iqbal was also assisted by his profound and regular study of the Holy Quran. For in the Book was the understanding of the eternal laws of happiness and disgrace, the advancement and decline of human groups and communities, and the revelation of the real causes of the events that take place in the world. In it also was such an accurate analysis of the processes of the growth and degeneration of nations that it baffles the intellect.

The only explanation is that this Book, which was revealed to an unlettered desert-dweller, is a programme for life that has been sent down by an all wise, all-knowing Being who is the Creator of the heavens and the earth. When Iqbal presented a copy of the Quran to King Nadir Shah of Afghanistan, he introduced it to him in these words:

> I said: It is the accumulated wisdom of men of Truth,
>   In its conscience dwells absolute life;
> Within it, the end of every beginning,
> By its lance, Ḥaydar is Khaliber's conqueror.

Similarly, in *Asrar-i-Khudi* ("Secrets of the Self") Iqbal writes;
> The Quran—the living Book,
> Recipe of the mysteries of life's origin.
> Its wisdom is infinite, eternal,
> By its power the impermanent is permanent.

The most illuminating and rewarding way to study Iqbal's works is aiming to discover the glimpses of history that are concealed in it and the lessons it contains for the students of human civilisation. In some of his stanzas and short poems and sometimes even in a single verse, he has, so to speak, poured whole oceans of history and philosophy of history into them. His ability to succinctly express what he means is miraculous. If the fundamental truths he has expounded in his poems were to be written in detailed prose with the necessary explanations and references, they would never be so effective and soul stirring. Their literary and historical worth and value and the far-reaching conclusions he has drawn from them can be fully appreciated only when one has a thorough grasp of history, particularly Islamic history, and is well acquainted with the spirit and significance of the Quran. It would also be necessary for one to have seriously studied Judaism, Christianity and the ancient Indian faiths as well as the philosophy and literature of Persia and of the Middle Ages, appropriately called the Dark Ages by Western writers.

Here we will present only a few examples of Iqbal's deep insight into history and wise understanding of the Quran. We have not searched for them through the whole of his works, nor attempted to examine them in all respects. They have been largely drawn from memory. In their explanation, reliance has been placed upon the learning of the average reader. In order to understand the significance of the events they indicate and the relevance and correctness of the observations made by Iqbal in respect of those happenings, it is essential to look into their background and the social and historical context in which they took place. Before reproducing the verses we will, therefore, describe briefly the facts and circumstances that inspired them.

Ancient religions, especially Christianity, had divided life into two watertight compartments—temporal and spiritual—and the world into "men of the world" and "men of faith" which were not only separate, but perpetually at war with each other. According to them, there was an intense rivalry between faith and the material world, and whoever chose one was compelled to give up the other and fight against it. No one, they asserted, could be both at the same time. Economic progress was not possible without the neglect of God-given laws, and power and rule could not be gained without giving up moral and religious precepts. In the same way, it was totally out of the question to think of piety and religiousness without renouncing the world and becoming a hermit.

Man, by nature, is easy going and any faith which frowned upon legitimate material pleasures and left no scope for worldly advancement or acquisition of power could never be acceptable to him. It was like waging war against his own personality and trying to crush his innate desires and emotions. The result was that a large number of intelligent and civilised men opted for the material world instead of faith and felt greatly satisfied with the decision. Having despaired of every kind of spiritual advancement, they directed their energies single-mindedly towards the pursuit of worldly aims and interests. Believing the contradiction between the material world and religion to be fundamental, different classes of men and institutions, by and large, said good-bye to faith. The State revolted against the Church and declared itself independent of its control. Thus, the government became power-drunk and society became wayward and perverse. The duality between the body and the soul and the rivalry between "men of religion" and "men of the world" not only weakened faith and morality and deprived the society of Divine favour, but also ushered in atheism. Europe was the first to fall prey to crude materialism, and to a greater or lesser extent, the other communities that came under the political, economic and intellectual influence of the West were also affected. The zealous exponents and preachers of Christian asceticism, according to whom nothing offered a greater hindrance to spiritual evolution than the state of being human, did the rest. They presented religion in a most revolting manner, and, in the name of it, sanctioned excesses. Consequently, there was a decline in moral and spiritual values and the world became ungodly and morally chaotic.[100]

The priceless gift of the Apostleship of the Prophet Muḥammad is the proclamation that deeds and morals of a man are, in truth, dependant upon *Niyah*.[101] According to Islam, neither religion nor the material world are absolute and independent. Even the greatest of worldly acts like government and warfare, the enjoyment of bodily pleasures and the earning of livelihood and leading a happy family life can become the sources of gaining the approval of God and attaining the highest grades of devoutness and spirituality. On the other hand, worship and acts of religion that are devoid of the aim of the approval of the Lord and are carried out with an attitude of negligence and indifference towards His commandments (as much as obligatory prayers and fundamental tenets of Islam like *Hijrah*,[102] *Jihād*,[103] sacrifice and *Dhikr* and *Tasbīḥ*) will be seen as purely worldly and undeserving of Divine recompense and reward. In fact, such a deed will, sometimes, be the cause of punishment and alienation from the Lord.[104]

The sacred Prophet removed the dualism of faith and material world and brought them together after centuries of mutual discord and distrust. He led mankind out of war with itself and made it do good, teaching it the comprehensive and revolutionary prayer, *Our Lord give us good in this world and good in the Hereafter, and defend us from the torment of the Fire* (QURAN, 2:201). By declaring, *Verily, my prayer and my sacrifice, and my life, and my death are for God, the Lord of the Worlds* (QURAN, 6:162), he established beyond doubt that the life of a truthful Believer was not a collection of so many different and mutually opposed units but a single unit of surrender and servitude. Here you will find dervishes in the garb of the world, ascetics in the robes of royalty and soldiers who are devotees by night and horsemen by day.

Now, after this brief introduction, read the poem of Iqbal entitled "Religion and Politics," and see how he has compressed within it everything including Christianity, Islam, the Middle Ages and the modern times. It is without doubt a masterpiece of profundity and charm.

> Foundation of the Church upon monasticism was laid,
> How could kingship in mendicancy be contained?
> Royalty and monkhood between them contended,
> It is exaltation, the other debasement,
> Politics freed itself from faith,
> Nothing did holiness of the old man of the Church avail,
> When separation took place between wealth and religion,
> All that was left was overlordship of desire,
> Duality is the misfortune of State and Religion,
> Duality is the benightedness of civilisation's eye,

It is the miracle of a desert-dweller,
Bearing of good tidings is synonymous with warning,
Safety of mankind in it lies,
That Sufi and King became one.[105]

The long history of the human race, a large part of which is taken up by the accounts of wars and conflicts, distinctly shows that it is power-drunkenness and the obsessive feeling of superiority rather than the concentration of power that has proved so disastrous for mankind. When an individual or community is seized with the idea that no one on earth is more powerful than him or it, and that the neighbouring peoples or the entire world is at his or its mercy he turns into a fearful force of destruction, and civilisations, moral values and fruits of the endeavours of religious mentors are wiped out. When the law of the jungle prevails humanity, justice, equality and ethics are empty, meaningless words and the fear of God, modesty and reverence for humanity are treated as signs of weakness and cowardice. What is still more distressing is that the hopes and aspirations for the reconstruction and advancement of mankind do then not rise again for hundreds of years. Towns and cities become deserted, places of worship are converted into wine-shops and gambling dens, and centres of learning are reduced to houses of fun and entertainment.

The Quran, in its own inimitable style, has drawn a vivid portrait of this mournful state of affairs in a short verse. By referring to the words uttered by the Queen of Sheba it has, in a way, set its seal to it. *Lo! Kings, when they enter a township, ruin it and make the honour of its people shame. Thus they will do* (QURAN, 27:34).

ʿĀd was one of the communities mentioned in the Quran that were noted in the past for arrogance and ostentation. It brought ruin and disaster to millions of fellow human beings and destroyed their fields and homes. *As for ʿĀd, they were arrogant in the land without right, and they said: "Who is mightier than us in power?" Could they not see that Allah, who created them, He is mightier* than them in power? And they denied our revelations (QURAN, 41:15).

This haughtiness, sensuality and ungodliness resulted in unrestrained use of power. The Prophet Hūd who was raised up among ʿĀd drew their attention to these vices. He said to them: *"Do you build on every high place a monument for vain delight? And do seek out strongholds that you may last forever? And when you apply force, you apply force as tyrants?"* (QURAN, 26:128-30). When an ungodly individual (or community) comes into absolute power anywhere, he begins to treat the weaker and less fortunate people with great disrespect. Of Pharaoh, the Quran says, *Lo! Pharaoh exalted himself in the earth and made its people castes. A tribe among them he oppressed, killing their sons and sparing their women. Lo! He was of those who work corruption* (QURAN, 28:4).

The Quran has drawn the portrait of an identical person who, in addition to being vain and self-centred, is a spellbinder with a smooth tongue. It is, in fact, not the description of an individual but of a whole class.

> And among people is he whose speech on the life of this world pleases you, and he calls to Allah to vouch for what is in his heart, yet he is the most virulent of opponents. And when he turns away [from thee], his effort in the land is to make mischief therein and to destroy the crops and the cattle; and Allah loves not mischief. And when it is said unto him, "Fear Allah," pride takes him to sin. Hell is sufficient for him, an evil resting-place. (QURAN, 2:204-6)

History is replete with examples of this mentality. During their time, the Romans and Persians were the most notable specimens of it. To quote from J.W. Draper's *History of the Conflict between Religion and Science*:

> Where the Empire, in a military and political sense, had reached its culmination, in a religious an social aspect, it had attained its height of immorality. It had become thoroughly Epicurean; its maxim was that life should be made a feast, that virtue is only the seasoning of pleasure, and temperance, the means of prolonging it. Dining-rooms glittering with gold and incrusted

with gems, slaves and superb apparel, the fascinations of feminine society where all the women were dissolute, magnificent baths, theatres, gladiators-such were the objects of Roman desire. The conquerors of the world had discovered that the only thing worth worshipping is force. By it all things might be secured, all that toil and trade had laboriously obtained. The confiscation of goods and lands, the taxation of provinces, were the reward of successful warfare, and the emperor was a symbol of force. There was a social splendour, but it was the phosphorescent corruption of the ancient Mediterranean world.[106]

Later, in the 17TH Century, came the semi-barbaric Tartars, the blood-curdling stories of whom are preserved in reliable history books like Ibn Kathīr's, *Al-Bidāyah wa'l-Nihāyah*. After a couple of victories they had become convinced that there was no one to check their advance in the surrounding world. It was a world-shaking calamity that rocked the foundations of the then civilised society. People were stricken with panic. Fear and despondency prevailed everywhere, an idea of which can be obtained not only from historical records, but also from the books on literature and mysticism as well.[107] These terrible men, "numerous as the ants and locusts," ravaged countries and razed beautiful cities to the ground. Dark clouds of destruction and death enveloped the Islamic world, which at that time was the leader of religion, morality and knowledge in the world. This had far reaching effects. Noble families of Iran, Afghanistan and Turkistan took refuge in India where the brave and sturdy Turks had established a flourishing Empire and could fight the Tartars on equal terms. Such an intellectual degeneration had set in the Islamic world and that some centres of learning sought safety in blocking the path of *ijtihād* and imitating them.[108]

Caesar, Alexander the Great, Chengiz, Halaku, Timur and Nadir Shah belonged to the same class of hunters of the human race. After reading the accounts of their dreadful exploits, read Iqbal's verses and see how he reconstructed this aspect of history.

> Many a time by the hands of Alexander and Chengiz,
> The robe of man has been torn to shreds;
> The eternal message of the history of nations is,
> O men of vision, intoxication of power is unsafe;
> Before this fast-moving, world-submerging torrent,
> Knowledge and understanding, arts and learning, are mere straw.

Many people in the East believe that today, in the 21ST Century, Europe and America are suffering from the same ailment of power-drunkenness and self-adulation. They have appointed themselves the guardians and protectors of men and the arbiters of their destiny. These Powers, too, are preoccupied with material gain and defend it with force. They do not allow a correctly guided leadership to emerge or survive in any part of the world.

The ruthless logic of gain and loss shows little respect for truth and justice and therefore does not permit Western leaders to think fairly and objectively on any issue concerning the East. They prefer to be aggressive against those who happen to be weak, even though justice is on the side of the weak. For this very reason, institutions like those set up by the United Nations are unable to live up to their professed intentions and serve the cause of universal peace, progress and freedom. Lack of sincerity has made the aid given by the Western countries to under-developed nations in the form of food, money and know-how completely ineffective. These gifts and grants offered to the Asian and African nations do not carry the moral weight that they should.

When power is directed towards a noble cause and made use of under the guidance of a fair-minded, God-fearing leader, it becomes a blessing and a source of life and growth. It is, then, employed to relieve the oppressed, to emancipate fellowmen, and to restore the true nature of mankind. Iqbal says:

> If [power be] ungodly, it is deadly poison,
> If in defence of faith an antidote against it.

In Iqbal's view, the Arab and Muslim conquerors made an

ideal example of the correct use of God-given power. They were thus able to deliver mankind from the over-lordship of fellow men to the over-lordship of God, and took man from the narrow confines and oppressiveness of the world to the fairness and justice of Islam. In the following lesser well-known verses, Iqbal has referred to the glorious achievements of the Arabs and the faith and message that inspired them to rise to those heights.[109]

> Touched by the breath of the unlettered One,
> The sands of Arabia began to throw up tulips.
> Freedom under his protection has been reared,
> The "today" of nations from his "yesterday" is.
> He put heart into the body of man,
> And from his face the veil he lifted.
> Every god of old he destroyed,
> Every withered branch by his moisture bloomed.
> The heat of the battles of Badr and Ḥunayn,
> Ḥaydar and Ṣiddīq, Farūq and Ḥusayn.
> In the thick of battle the majesty of *Adhān*,
> The recitation of *al-Ṣaffāt*[110] at the point of sword.
> The scimitar of Ayyūb, the glance of Bayazīd,
> Key to the treasures of this world and the next.
> Ecstasy of heart and mind from the same wine-cup,
> Fusion of Rūmī's devotion and Rāzī's thought.
> Knowledge and wisdom, faith and law, government and politics,
> Hearts in breasts devoid of peace.
> Al-Hamara and Taj of breath-taking beauty,
> To which even the angels pay tribute.
> These, too, a fragment of his priceless bequest,
> Of his countless glimpses only a glimpse.
> His exterior these enthralling sights,
> Of his interior even the knowing unaware.
> Boundless praise be to the sacred Apostle,
> Who imparted faith to a handful of dust.

It is an accepted fact that those who laid the foundations of mighty empires were virile and sturdy men. They led an austere and rugged life, free from every kind of self-indulgence and it is because of their efforts backward and downtrodden people attained eminence. On account of this hardiness, high-mindedness and enterprise, they succeeded in setting up empires, under most unfavourable circumstances, which flourished for centuries. However, profusion of riches, unwholesome environments, selfish and greedy courtiers and shameless sycophants gradually exerted their influence on those who came after them, and they grew lazy, slothful and ease loving. Instead of seeking glory in the field of battle, they revelled in luxury and amusement. Far from concentrating on the defence of their lands and making new conquests, their time and energies were spent on material pleasures and the gratification of animal desires. It is hard to find an exception to the above-mentioned principle of history. It appears to be as inexorable as the law of nature, and can correctly be described as the logical outcome of a long period of affluence and power. The Quran has put this truth into words: *Nay, but verily man becomes rebellious, when he thinketh himself self-sufficient* (QURAN, 96:6-7).

If you study anyone's career you will find the confirmation of the same principle in the story of their rise and fall. You will be struck by the same difference in the morals, lifestyles and social and moral standards of the founders of powerful kingdoms and their successors.

We will, therefore, confine ourselves to citing only two examples that are related to the community which is expected to be the foremost exponent of moral teachings in the world and whose Prophet tied stones to his stomach (to subdue the pangs of hunger) thus taking pride in poverty.

Everyone knows what the state of the Arabs was when they came out of their Peninsular home to spread the message of Islam and extend the "Kingdom of God" over the whole of the earth. They were courageous and their lifestyle was disciplined. Like true soldiers and ascetics they practised severe self-denial and kept strictly away from bodily enjoyment. They established great empires by means of the all-conquering force of Islam and the glowing qualities of their mind and character. One of these was the Abbasid Kingdom, with its capital at Baghdad, which dominated almost half of the then civilised world for about five hundred years in the name of Islamic Caliphate. Until Hārūn and Ma'mūn, its founders and early rulers were virile and sturdy men, accustomed to the disciplined life of soldiers.[111] However, after a time, the Abbasid Empire started to break up and its rulers, who still bore relation to the Islamic Caliphate, became lovers of ease and luxury. Thus, a tremendous wave of high living, ungodliness and sensuality swept over Baghdad which did not spare even those noted for sobriety and learning. From the capital, the craze for extracting the maximum pleasure from life extended to the other towns and blind gratification of one's inclinations and desires became the order of the day. The outcome of excessive sensuality and heedlessness appeared in the form of the Tartar invasion during the reign of the last of the Abbasid Caliphs, Muʿtaṣim Billah, and the centre of learning and culture became immersed in bloodshed.[112]

A renowned historian, Qutubuddin Norwhali has summed up the state of the citizens of Baghdad during the time of Muʿtaṣim as follows: "Cosy in the warm and soft meadows on the outskirts of Baghdad, players on the flute of ease and repose, accustomed to the stream and garden, surrounded all the time by friends and admirers, their table-spread (on which food was laid) full of fruit and drink; they never had anything to do with fighting, nor had their mouth and palate ever tasted the bitterness of war."[113]

Secondly, the Mughul Empire of India which was founded by Ẓahīruddīn Babar (1482-1530) possessed good solid foundations, which had been laid with a feeling of earnest repentance and citizens resolved to abstain from sinful ways, and act upon courage and purpose.

When Babar, who was in a foreign land, saw that he had only

200,00 soldiers to meet the 1,000,000 strong army of Rana Sanga he realised he could not hope for reinforcements and he chose an original way to victory. Abu al-Qasim Farishta writes:

> After a little thought and hesitation, the one whose abode is Paradise said, "What will the Muslim rulers of the world think of this cowardice of mine? Evidently, they all will feel that in order to save my life, I gave up such a large and extensive country. I believe, it is better to keep in mind the blessed goal of martyrdom and exert with my heart and soul in the field of Battle." The people who were present heard the King's speech, and, with one voice, the cry of *Jihād* was raised from every corner. The King's speech produced such effect on the hearts that everyone, bowing his head in submission said, "What good fortune can be more attractive than martyrdom. It is apparent that the motto of Muslims is that if we slay, we are *Ghāzīs* [Heroes] and if we are slain we are *Shahīd* [Martyrs]. We swear according to the *Sharī'ah* [Muslim Sacred Law] that we shall not even think of withdrawing from the battlefield." The nobles, further, strengthened their promise and assurance with oath. The King, who was never without wine and cupbearer, gave up drinking altogether in response to the need of the hour. He also resolved earnestly to abstain from all acts that are forbidden and even *makrūh* [acts that are not forbidden by considered reprehensible] even the shaving of beard.[114]

How did such an Empire raised up the foundations of bravery, resoluteness and solemn undertaking to the Almighty end up taking the path of ruin when its determined and fearless successors included the enlightened rulers like Humayun, Akbar and Aurangzeb? An idea of the degeneration can be imagined from the account of the life and character of Mohammad Shah (1719-1748), popularly known as *Rangiley* (man of pleasure), and the revelries and vulgar festivities that took place in his Court.

NOTES

1. *Na't* is a poem in praise of the Holy Prophet. *Na't-goi* is the art of writing it.
2. *Milad* literally means "birth" or "birthday." Among the Muslims the term is applied to an oration or discourse on the birth and doings of the Prophet. *Milad Nama* is the book containing it and *Milad-Khwan* is the narrator thereof.
3. The title of the Urdu version of the book.
4. The title of the Arabic version.
5. An elegy, particularly one written or recited in commemoration of the martyrdom of Ḥusayn and his companions at Karbala.
6. The name of Ḥusayn.
7. *Kalim* is the name of Moses. *Kalimi*, here, can be said to denote Moseshood.
8. Meaning the Public Treasury or Exchequer, into which payment on various accounts is made, and according to the sources from which they are derived, applicable to the support of different classes of persons.
9. Entitled *Risalatul Mashriq* and *Zarb-el-Kalim*. Dr. Azzam has also rendered into Arabic some portions of *Asrar-i-Khudi*, *Rumuz-i-Bekhudi* and *Javed Nama*.
10. It can also be translated as "to his son Javid."

11. The sacred enclosure at Makkah.

12. Meaning Western or European according to the circumstances.

13. Denoting Prophet Ibrāhīm (Abraham) who was thrown into the fire at the command of Nimrud.

14. The reference is to the story of the pulpit that wept when it was changed and the sacred Prophet did not lean on it.

15. A rationalising philosopher who is often placed by Iqbal in antithesis to Rūmī.

16. *Kashshāf* (meaning the Key), which has been used in the original, is the title of a well-known commentary of the Quran. It was written by Allama Zamakhshri.

17. Iqbal uses the Qalandar as a symbol for the evolved man who has realised in himself the truths of self-development.

18. The name of a river of Turkistan.

19. The word ʿ*Ajam*, frequently used by Iqbal, signifies what is foreign, i.e not Arabian or purely Islamic.

20. The *Saqi*, as V.G. Kierman remarks, was originally the page or cupbearer of the Arabs, and later the hetaira of the Persians, the mistress who pours the wine. From the common symbolism of wine as truth, love as inspiration, the *Saqi*, the filler of the spiritual cup, comes to mean the leader, spiritual guide or even God. The word is often used ambiguously in poetry.

21. Names of Idols worshipped by pagan Arabs.

22. The sacred enclosure of the House of Kaʿba at Makkah.

23. Prophet Abraham (Ibrāhīm ﷺ).

24. The father of Abraham.

25. Meaning, *There is no God save the One God*.

26. ʿAlī ibn Abī Ṭālib.

27. A prince of Iran who, leaving his all, went to Arabia, embraced Islam and became a companion of the Prophet.

28. A kind of verse in which the meaning of the first verse of each stanza is completed in the last.
29. Name of a region near the source of Oxus, famous for its rubies.
30. This refers to the Prophet ﷺ.
31. Kneeling and touching the forehead to the ground in Muslim ritual Prayer.
32. Standing erect in Prayer.
33. The allusion is to the Muslim confession of faith meaning, "There is no god except One God."
34. Ayaz was the favourite slave and inmate of Mahmud of Ghazna.
35. The call of *Allāhu Akbar*.
36. *Jal-tarang* is the music produced by filling a brass vessel with water and beating the edges with two sticks. What Iqbal means is that the music of life is produced by filling its vessel with *Lahu* (blood), not water.
37. The kings of Persia of the Kayanian dynasty.
38. Mount Sinai on which Moses witnessed the effects of Divine epiphany. The name of a famous Persian statuary, who, to please his mistress, Shirin, hewed his way through a mountain and caused a stream of milk to flow along a canal.
39. The title of Hazrat ʿAlī.
40. Rustam son of Zal (nicknamed Dastan) was a famous hero of pre-Islamic Persia.
41. The name of a hill in Makkah.
42. A Companion of the sacred Prophet who used to give the *Adhān* in his mosque.
43. The Heroes of Islam.
44. Meaning the religious teacher.

45. Meaning earnest and ceaseless striving for a noble cause, involving sacrifice of both life and property.
46. Farhad's beloved who typifies feminine charm and sweetness.
47. The king, in the legend of Farhad, who symbolises despotism.
48. Circumambulation of the House of Kaʿba.
49. The maker of the Golden Calf.
50. Ablution performed before Prayer.
51. Alms that Muslims must pay from their earnings.
52. Meaning the fighter in the defence of true faith.
53. A district of Tartary. Famous for musk.
54. Abū Lahab was the name of one of the Prophet's most bitter enemies.
55. Son of Hazrat ʿAlī and grandson of the Holy Prophet, who became a martyr at the battle of Karbala in 680 CE.
56. Title of sura 37 of the Quran. It means "Those Who Sot The Ranks."
57. *Hadi* is the song the camel drivers of Arabia sing whilst leading a caravan. *Hadi Khwan* means the singer of Hadi.
58. The term *Millet-i-Marhoom* used in the original means the community on which God may have mercy. It denotes the Muslims.
59. Invocation to God to bestow his choicest favours and blessings on the Prophet.
60. Meaning *He is God*.
61. An enemy of the Prophet ﷺ.
62. The "Helpers" who were the original inhabitants of Yathrib (Madinah).
63. *Iqbal Nama*, p. 27.
64. *Iqbal Nama*, p. 446..

65. *Iqbal Nama*, p. 452.
66. A famous poet during the time of Mahmud Ghaznavi. He started with lyrical poetry and rose to be the court poet of the Sultan. However, when awakening came to him he retired from the world and began to write only mystical and philosophical poems.
67. The doctrine that there is only One God.
68. It signifies the Manṣūr who was put to death for believing in the identity of the individual soul with the Divine spirit and raising the cry of *God is I!*
69. Repeating the names, praises and attributes of God.
70. Repeating phrases of worship, particularly *subḥān'Allāh*.
71. Circumambulation around the Kaʿba in Makkah.
72. Batha is the name of the valley in Makkah.
73. Europe.
74. The allusion here is to the prayer of Noah reproduced earlier.
75. A *Mathnawi* is a long poem in which the couplets rhyme regularly, as one finds in English heroic verse.
76. The name of an uncle of the Prophet who was one of his most stubborn enemies. He was killed in the battle of Badr in A.D 623.
77. Ancient idols of Arabia.
78. Public crier to prayer.
79. Makhzūm was the name of Abū Jahl's tribe and he was its leader.
80. Hatīm is the name of a portion of land in the north of Kaʿba that was left out when the Kaʿba was rebuilt.
81. Mudhir was the name of a famous tribe of the Quraysh.
82. The Prophet's father was named ʿAbdullāh.
83. ʿAdnān was the founder of a large Arab group of tribes, hence

	legendary ancestor of the Arab people.
84.	A famous Arab orator.
85.	The name of a celebrated pre-Islamic poet.
86.	"The day primordial." Literally means *Am I not?* As described in the Quran, 7:172.
87.	Ahriman was the god of evil and Yazdan the god of good among the ancient Iranians.
88.	Jamāluddīn Afghānī (1838-1897) was one of the leading figures in the 19th century revivalist movement and a pioneer of Islamic unity.
89.	Sa'id Halim Pasha (1838-1914) was a prominent Ottoman statesman.
90.	Money lent without interest and repaid at the convenience of the borrower.
91.	An act of charity, which is of lasting benefit.
92.	The song leader of the caravan.
93.	The place in the Prophet's Mosque at Madinah where one stands "face to face" with him.
94.	Madinah.
95.	Famous Persian poets, whose poems in praise of the Prophet are highly popular among Muslims.
96.	*Mulla* is the self-styled priest of Islam which, as a religion, recognises no priesthood.
97.	Ascetic.
98.	No one is all-powerful save Allah.
99.	The allusion is to Ṣalāḥuddīn.
100.	J.W. Draper: *History of the Conflict between Religion and Science.* Also the author's *Islam and the World.*
101.	Even the opening words of the tradition, which Bukhari has placed at the head of his compilation, are: "Behold, the actions

are (but) judged according to the intentions; and, behold, unto every man is due what he intended." According to many authorities, it comprises one third of Islam.

102. Migration for the sake of God.
103. Holy War.
104. Numerous traditions in support of it are found in the standard collections.
105. *Baal-I-Jibril.*
106. See pp. 31-32.
107. A greater light has been shed on it in the author's *Tarikh-i-Dawat-o-Azimat*, 1:393-404.
108. Iqbal has offered the same explanation of the closing of the door of Itj*ihād* by the Muslim theologians in the 8TH Century.
109. *Pas Che Bayid Kard*, p. 53.
110. Title of the 37th chapter (or sura) of the Quran.
111. Details are given in the author's *Al-Mado Jazr Fi Tarikh-ul-Islam.*
112. Details are given in the author's *Tarikh-i-Dawat-o-Azimat.*
113. *Al-A'alam Ba-A'alam Bait-ullah-ul-Harem*, p. 180.
114. *Tarikh-I-Farishta* (Urdu version), Hyderabad, 1926, p. 219.